WILLIAM BRADFORD
Rock of Plymouth

WILLIAM BRADFORD
Rock of Plymouth

KIERAN DOHERTY

Twenty-First Century Books
Brookfield, Connecticut

To my mother, Mary, who made me believe;
and my wife, Lynne, who made this possible.

Photographs courtesy of North Wind Picture Archives: pp. 30, 58, 59;
The Granger Collection, New York: pp. 43, 76, 86; Corbis-Bettmann: p. 96;
Archive Photos: p. 142; The Bostonian Society: p. 157

Library of Congress Cataloging-in-Publication Data
Doherty, Kieran.
William Bradford : rock of Plymouth / Kieran Doherty.
p.   cm.
Includes bibliographical references and index.
Summary: A biography of one of the founders of the Plymouth Colony
in Massachusetts and a history of the Pilgrims' difficult times during
their early years in the New World.
ISBN 0-7613-1304-4 (lib. bdg.)
1. Bradford, William, 1588–1657–Juvenile literature. 2. Pilgrims
(New Plymouth Colony)–Biography–Juvenile literature. 3. Governors–
Massachusetts–Biography–Juvenile literature. 4. Massachusetts–History–New
Plymouth, 1620–1691–Juvenile literature. 5. Plymouth (Mass.)–Biography–
Juvenile literature. [1. Bradford, William, 1588-1657. 2. Governors.
3. Pilgrims (New Plymouth Colony) 4. Massachusetts–History–
New Plymouth, 1620–1691.] I. Title.
F68.B8235D64   1999
974.4'02'092–dc21
[B]   99-10631   CIP   AC

Published by Twenty-First Century Books
A Division of The Millbrook Press, Inc.
2 Old New Milford Road
Brookfield, Connecticut 06804

CONTENTS

❧ PREFACE ❧

Several years ago I had occasion to read *Of Plymouth Plantation*, William Bradford's famous history of the Pilgrims and the settlement they founded in America in 1620. As I read that book, I realized that almost everything I had ever known about the Pilgrims as a student was either wrong or, at best, half-right. With that realization I knew I wanted to tell the true story of William Bradford and the Pilgrims of Plymouth.

In this book I try to tell that story. In the process I hope I have brought William Bradford and the other Pilgrims to life. I hope I have changed them from the plaster saints of myth and legend into the living, breathing, often courageous, sometimes foolish men and women they were as they set out to establish the first permanent English colony north of Virginia.

To write this story, I have found it necessary to quote extensively from William Bradford's writings, particularly *Of Plymouth Plantation*. There is, in fact, almost no other original research material available about the Pilgrims and their colony. While several editions of this book are available, I chose to use the most recent edition, edited by the notable American historian Samuel Eliot Morison. In this edition Bradford's original language was recast so that it might be more easily understood by a modern reader without the loss of its original power and poetry.

Unfortunately, William Bradford was a private man. Though he wrote extensively about the Pilgrims' trials and occasional victories, both in Europe and in America, he wrote little about his own role in the founding of Plymouth and nothing about his feelings or thoughts. More than once, as I was writing this book, I wished that I could somehow travel back almost four centuries in time to sit with Bradford at the dining table in his house in Plymouth and ask him questions, tug his beard, so to speak, to force him to reveal more about his life as a man. Since that was impossible, I used my own common sense–backed by research–to add "flesh" to William Bradford's character. In no case, however, did I fictionalize Bradford's life, and when I was forced to make fact-based assumptions I took pains to make that tactic clear in the text.

About dates in this book: William Bradford and his contemporaries used what we know today as the Old Style calendar. According to this calendar, the new year began on March 25 instead of January 1. That means that what Bradford called February of 1625 was actually February of 1626. At the same time, this Old Style calendar did not take into account the effect of leap years, so that the date Bradford knew as December 11 we would figure as December 21 according to our New Style calendar.

Throughout this book the days of the month are dated according to the Old Style calendar, while the years are dated according to the New Style calendar.

❧ 1 ❧

BIRTH AND BOYHOOD

"We have noted these things, that you may
see the worth of these things, and not
negligently lose what your fathers have
obtained with so much hardship...." [1]

William Bradford was born in March 1590 in the farming village of Austerfield, in Yorkshire, about 150 miles (240 kilometers) north of London. While the exact date of his birth is not known, the Austerfield parish register does contain an entry that "William sone of William Bradfourth" was baptized on March 19 of that year. Since about one of every four babies born died soon after birth in those days, most parents saw to it that infants were christened within days of entering the world.

William's father was a yeoman, a gentleman farmer who earned more than 40 pounds (a fairly substantial amount of money in 1590) from his landholdings each year. As a yeoman, he was a man of substance in the rural village of Austerfield. He had the right to vote and to run for elective office. William's mother, Alice, was the daughter of the town's leading merchant.

As one of the more prosperous families in the village, the Bradfords—young Will, as he was surely called, his older sister Alice, born in about 1587, and his mother and father—almost certainly lived in a roomy, comfortable house. Though we don't know what that house was like, it was probably built of local stone and not the mud-daubed twigs and sticks used in the construction of the poorest of peasant cottages. Meals were cooked in the main room's fireplace, large enough to hold a side of beef. The meat, bread, cheese, wine, and ale that were the mainstays of a typical Elizabethan country diet were eaten at a rough table where Alice Bradford, the children, and any guests who might happen by sat on long benches called "forms." Will's father, as the "chairman" of the family, sat in a chair at the head of the table.

While the Bradford family was relatively well off, Will's mother and father spent long hours every day hard at work. Will's father rose before dawn and was in the fields at daybreak. He spent his day tending sheep, which were sold for income, and the few cattle he kept for meat and milk. When not caring for his livestock, he worked in the family garden, where he grew cabbages, turnips, radishes, and other vegetables that added variety to the daily menu. At night, he sat by the flickering light of an open-flame oil lamp or a candle making or mending tools for use in the fields.

Alice Bradford, too, worked from sunup to sundown and beyond. As the children crawled and played on the rush-strewn floor of the great room, she combed and carded wool shorn from the family's sheep, cooked and cleaned, made butter and cheese, and at day's end, mended and sewed, and, no doubt, fell into bed each night grateful for her sleep.

If Will's circumstances had not changed drastically when he was still just an infant, this simple, rural life probably would have been his destiny. He would almost certainly have grown up to be a farmer like his father. In early July 1591, however, when Will was just one year old, his father died, probably the victim of smallpox or dysentery or one of the other deadly illnesses common in those times.

When he was four years of age, Will, who was destined to gain fame as a Pilgrim Father, became something of a pilgrim in his own land. His mother remarried, and Will was sent to live with his grandfather, also named William Bradford. Then, in 1596, his grandfather died, and Will returned home to live with his mother and stepfather. That period, too, was brief, for about a year later his mother died, and Will, then aged seven, was sent to live with his uncles, Robert and Thomas Bradford, on a nearby farm.

It was also about this time that Will was struck with what Cotton Mather, the famous Puritan minister and historian who wrote a biography of William Bradford, called a "soon and long sickness."[2] Since the evidence of William Bradford's later life shows that he was a strong, healthy man, even when he faced the terrible rigors of life on the New England frontier, the sickness that struck him soon after he moved to his uncles' farm was likely more psychological than physical. This wouldn't be surprising. After all, he suffered through the deaths of his father, grandfather, and mother—all in the space of just a few years. At only seven years of age, it must have seemed to him that he had been abandoned by everyone he loved and trusted.

Meanwhile, perhaps because his illness prevented him from doing hard work on the farm, or perhaps because his uncles realized he would be more valuable if he could read and write, they sent Will to school, probably when he was about eight years old.

Going to school in those days was not much fun. Classes started early in the morning and lasted until late in the day. For long hours, students sat on hard benches reciting lessons over and over, learning a little religion and reading and basic mathematics. Students were expected to sit still and behave. The use of the "rod" was common.

Bradford probably learned his letters using a piece of wood on which the alphabet, the vowel sounds, and the prayer known as the "Our Father" had been inscribed. Fitted with a handle and covered with a protective sheet of horn, this so-called ABC or hornbook would have served as his only textbook. Once he mastered the ABCs he would have been taught a little mathematics, perhaps not much more than how to count. His teacher also would have taught him social skills, again by rote, perhaps using this verse common in Bradford's time.

First, I command thee God to serve,
then to thy parents duty yield:
Unto all men be courteous,
and mannerly in town and field.

Your clothes unbuttoned do not use,
let not your hose ungartered be;
Have handkerchief in readiness,
wash hands and face, or see not me.[3]

It appears likely that Will not only applied himself to his lessons but found someone—perhaps a friendly clergyman—to further his education and provide him with books, for by the time he was twelve his reading level was beyond anything he could have achieved in a typical school. "When he was about a Dozen Years Old," Cotton Mather said, "the Reading of the Scriptures began to cause great Impressions upon him."[4] In all likelihood, he was reading the Holy Scriptures and *The Book of Martyrs*, one of the most popular religious books of that time.

By 1602, according to Mather, Will had become a serious student of the Bible and was introduced to the religious movement known as Puritanism. This changed the course of his life and, eventually, the course of history. In order to understand William Bradford and his life, it is necessary to know just a bit about Puritanism and one of its offshoots, known as Separatism.

Puritanism was the outgrowth of a controversy that swept across England in 1536. In that year, King Henry VIII, then a member of the Roman Catholic Church, decided he wanted to divorce his wife, Catherine of Aragon, in hopes that the younger Anne Boleyn might become his wife and provide him with an heir. When Henry applied to the pope for permission to divorce, however, the pope denied his request. Not used to having his will thwarted, Henry ultimately left the Catholic Church, founded the Anglican Church, established himself as its leader, and made it the state religion of England.

Henry's actions threw England into turmoil, which grew worse after he died and his daughter Mary took the throne. A staunch Catholic, Mary was determined to force her subjects—many of whom had become comfortable as Anglicans—back to the Catholic Church. To accomplish this end, she ordered the death of hundreds of Anglicans for no crime other than their faith, earning herself the name "Bloody Mary."

By the time of William Bradford's birth, Mary was long dead. Elizabeth I, another of Henry's daughters, was queen. The nation was once again Anglican. The established church, however, was itself in turmoil. Many of its members believed that their church was too much like the Catholic Church, which they now hated, thanks, at least in part, to Mary's bloodthirsty ways.

These unhappy Anglicans wanted the Church of England, as it was also known, to be cleansed of any taint of Catholicism. They wanted a simpler faith, with churches like those in the earliest days of Christianity. They wanted to do away with bishops and all the sacraments except for baptism and communion. They wanted their churches to be simple, without candles and fancy robes and the statues and crucifixes that decorated Catholic church buildings. Since these nonconformist Anglicans wanted to cleanse or "purify" their church, they became known as "Puritans."

By the early sixteenth century, many Puritans had banded together to form their own congregations. Although these men and women disliked much about the Anglican Church, they were unwilling to leave it completely. They believed they would eventually change the church from within.

Meanwhile, there was another, even more radical, religious group in England. This group believed virtually the same things the Puritans did, but that the Anglican Church would never change and they had no choice but to leave. These men and women took to heart the preaching of the Apostle Paul, who said, "Come out from among them, and be separate from them, says the Lord, and touch nothing unclean; then I will welcome you."[5] Since they turned their backs on the Anglican faith, they were widely known as "Separatists."

Like so much of Bradford's life, the exact story of how he made his way to his first Puritan service is lost in the shadows of the distant past. We do know, however, that when he was about twelve years old, he and another boy about the same age walked 8 miles (13 kilometers) or so from Austerfield to the village of Babworth. There, in a service probably held in a private home or in an open field, he heard a famous minister, Richard Clyfton, preach in the simple Puritan way. Whatever Clyfton said, it changed young William Bradford's life. From that day forward, he began what Cotton Mather described as a "Holy, Prayerful, Watchful and Fruitful Walk with God."[6]

How could a single Puritan meeting change Will's life so drastically? Perhaps he had already come to believe that the pomp and circumstance of the Anglican Church was a hindrance to a true relationship between God and man. Many other men and women in England had come to the same conclusion. Perhaps, also, the reason had less to do with God and more to do with Will's human relatives. It is conceivable that Will, who until this time had regularly attended Anglican services with his uncles, was only looking for a way to rebel. If that was his motivation, however, it was strong enough to last him a lifetime. It appears more likely that Will found at that first Puritan meeting a faith that enabled him to have a more personal contact with his Creator, a faith that moved him as the Anglican faith never had. So, Sunday after Sunday, Will walked to Babworth to hear Clyfton and to associate with others who believed as he did. He continued even after the young friend who introduced him to Puritanism turned away from his new faith.

William Bradford was only a Puritan for a short time when events transpired in London that were to move him and many other Puritans in England even further from the Anglican Church. On March 3, 1603, Queen Elizabeth I died in her sleep, to be succeeded by King James I. At first, the Puritans were filled with hope that James would force the Anglican Church to change. Almost immediately, however, the new king let it be known he had no intention of changing the Anglican faith. Following one meeting with a group of nonconformist leaders pleading for change, he said of the Puritans, "I shall make them conform themselves, or I will harry them out of the land."[7]

As news of the king's anti-Puritan stance spread through the land, many Puritans left the church completely to become Separatists. Among them was William Bradford, who, in about 1606, joined a newly formed Separatist congregation that met in the tiny village of Scrooby, about 2 miles (3 kilometers) from Austerfield. These Scrooby Separatists, as history has named them, held their meetings in Scrooby Manor, which was tenanted by William Brewster, a forty-year-old Cambridge graduate whose past service to the crown had gained him a position as district postmaster, responsible for the King's Mail and for the operation of a small inn or tavern housed in the manor.

Separatist congregations, including the one that met at Scrooby Manor, were formed around what its members called a "covenant." This was a holy contract, or vow, that the members of the congregation made with God and with each other to protect and care for each other while they lived their lives in accordance with the teachings of the New Testament.

Since they had openly turned their backs on the official state religion of England, these Separatists were forced to practice their faith in secret, knowing that just by praying together they risked imprisonment. Because of their shared faith and the dangers they faced together, the Scrooby Separatists were a tight-knit group, a kind of a one-for-all-and-all-for-one community.

One doesn't have to be a psychologist to understand how membership in this close-knit group would have affected an orphaned teenager like William Bradford. Without a doubt, when seventeen-year-old William joined the Scrooby congregation he must have felt that he was part of a real family. In the group he also found a father figure in William Brewster. Well educated and well traveled, Brewster was an elder of the congregation and, hence, an authority figure that Will could look up to. More than that, though, he was a warm and caring man.

Brewster, for his part, must have seen in William a boy worth fathering. Perhaps he saw in him a young man he could shape, help educate, and make ready for the service of God.

In any case, Brewster took William under his wing. He made him a member of his household, probably employing him as a secretary or assistant. He also lent him books, tutored him in Latin, and taught him how to think critically. It is easy to imagine the man and boy sitting together late at night in one of the manor's drafty rooms discussing religion, the world beyond Scrooby, the meaning of life itself.

There is no doubt that the times he and Brewster shared in Scrooby were very important for the fatherless Bradford. The boy grew to love and respect the man who became the greatest influence on his life. Writing about Brewster years later, he called him "my dear and loving friend . . . tenderhearted and compassionate. . . ."[8]

By the age of seventeen, then, William Bradford had found in the Separatist congregation a feeling of family—a happiness, a sense of belonging and well-being that, in all likelihood, he had never known before.

All too soon, though, this happy period of William Bradford's life was to come to an end.

2

AN ADVENTURE
ALMOST DESPERATE

"...Seeing themselves thus molested, and that there
was no hope of their continuance there, by a joint
consent they resolved to go into [Holland], where
they heard was freedom of religion for all men...."[1]

Being a religious dissident in England in William
Bradford's time was a dangerous business. The prisons
of England held scores of men and women whose only
crime was practicing a faith other than Anglicanism.
Many of these dissidents were confined for months or
years without ever being brought to trial. They were
held in terrible conditions, William Bradford said, "per-
ishing by cold, hunger, or [the] noisomeness of the
prison."[2]

While William and the other Separatists who met
each week in William Brewster's house were able to
avoid official persecution, they did suffer at the hands
of their neighbors and—at least in Bradford's case—their
family members.

Mather called those who persecuted the Separatists "a most ignorant and licentious people."[3] The truth is that the conformists who harassed Bradford and the other Separatists were neither evil nor stupid. They were simple rural men and women, members of the Anglican Church who couldn't understand why the Separatists would turn their backs on England's established religion. Like most people in other times and places, the conformists of the Scrooby district simply reacted with fear and anger when they were confronted by people who were different.

At the age of just sixteen or seventeen, Bradford must have felt terrible when the people of Scrooby–people he had known his whole life–jeered and taunted him or turned away in scorn when they saw him on the village streets. He must have felt lonely and despairing when, as Mather said, he suffered "the wrath of his uncles" because of his conversion.[4] Perhaps it was these experiences that made Bradford a remarkably tolerant man, then and in later life.

The conformists who lived in and around Scrooby, most of the population, were not the only ones who feared and resented the Saints, as the Separatists called themselves to signify they were members of God's true church. King James I and later King Charles I both viewed the Separatists as dangerous because they practiced democracy in religion (electing their own church leaders) and questioned the king's supremacy in church affairs. Anglican priests, believing their authority was under attack by the nonconformists, soon counterattacked. They used their pulpits, week after week, to preach against the Scrooby group and other dissidents.

Separatists, one of these clerics charged from his pulpit, were "proud . . . presumptuous . . . holy without religion . . . dangerous and malicious Hypocrite[s]."[5] In preaching against the Separatists, the priests gave what amounted to official approval to their persecution by their neighbors. This was no small matter in a time when public pronouncements from church pulpits had as much power to form opinion as television and newspapers do today.

Although the Scrooby Saints were harassed by their neighbors during the early months of 1607, it appears that the congregation was not—as yet—persecuted by either the civil or church authorities. In all likelihood, the king's officers and the bishops of the Anglican Church were not seriously concerned about a small group of dissidents in a hamlet far from London.

Still, from what Bradford later wrote, we know that he and the other Separatists in rural Yorkshire were aware that their fellow dissenters in London were being sorely persecuted. They knew as well that the exercise of their beliefs could easily lead to the same punishments. These facts, coupled with the persecution they suffered at the hands of the conformists, soon convinced them they would have to flee from England if they wished to live in peace and safety.

In the late spring or early summer of 1607, the members of the church met—probably in the main hall of Scrooby Manor—to decide about their future. One who almost certainly took a leading role in discussions about what the Separatists should do was John Robinson, a Cambridge graduate who joined the group soon after it was formed and quickly became its "teacher," or assistant minister.

Described by Bradford as a "famous and worthy man,"[6] Robinson would serve for many years as the spiritual guide for the people we know as the Pilgrims.

We can be sure that he was one of the group's strongest leaders from its very early days.

In any case, after what must have been hours of discussion and argument, the Scrooby Separatists determined—probably by a vote of all adult males—to flee from England and to "go into the Low Countries, where they heard was freedom of religion for all men."[7] The Low Countries was the name then used to describe the Netherlands, a low-lying region almost surrounded by the sea and crisscrossed by rivers and man-made canals.

It is difficult for us today to imagine the courage it took for the Saints to decide to leave England. Virtually none of these men and women had ever been more than a few miles from their rural homes. Crossing the North Sea to Amsterdam meant turning their backs on the only world they had ever known, almost certainly never to return. The move to Holland, Bradford wrote, "was by many thought an adventure almost desperate; a case intolerable and a misery worse than death."[8]

Their own fears were not the only barriers that the Saints had to overcome. Since government approval was required for all travel abroad and this was automatically denied to religious dissenters, the Separatists would have to sneak out of the country, like thieves.

The Saints quickly began selling what possessions they could to raise money for their voyage. They packed books and clothing and a few household items. Finally, in late 1607 or early 1608, Bradford and about one hundred other men, women, and children bound for Amsterdam made their way on foot some 60 miles (97 kilometers) to the old city of Boston, on England's southeast coast. There, they were to be met by a ship that would carry them to Holland.

This first attempt at escape ended in disaster when the ship's captain, who was supposed to be their savior, instead turned the Separatists over to customs officers in exchange for a reward. Bradford and the other Saints were arrested, but not before the king's men "rifled and ransacked them . . . ,"[9] stripping men and women to their underclothes, stealing their money, books, and any other valuables they could find.

Following their arrests, Bradford and the other Saints were thrown in jail, where they were kept while the authorities in Boston awaited instructions from London. Apparently the authorities were not worried about a ragtag group of dissidents in far-off Boston. Within a few months, all were released.

After this escape attempt, Bradford and the others returned to Scrooby, where they found shelter with family members and friends as they waited for another chance to flee. In mid-1608, they tried again, making their way across central England to a lonely bay not far from the port city of Hull, where they were to be met by a Dutch sea captain who had agreed to carry them all to Holland. At the appointed time, the women and children in the group were in a small boat, hidden in a creek that emptied into the bay. The men, including Bradford, stood on the beach, keeping watch.

Unluckily, by the time the Dutch vessel appeared, the tide had dropped and the small boat containing the women and children was hard aground. Shouts rang out from the Dutch ship urging the men to come aboard, where they could wait for the tide to rise. About half the men were on board when, suddenly, the Dutch captain spied a large mob approaching. There were, Bradford said, "both horse and foot, with bills and guns and other weapons, for the country was raised to take them."[10]

The Dutch captain knew that if he tried to rescue those still on shore, all would be arrested. In the hands of the English he would lose his ship and, perhaps, his life. He had no choice other than to flee. He ordered his ship's anchor raised and her sails unfurled. In minutes, the vessel was bearing away from shore, bound for Holland.

"The poor men which were got aboard were in great distress for their wives and children which they saw thus to be taken," Bradford said. The women and children on the shore, he added, were "pitiful . . . to see . . . weeping and crying on every side, some for their husbands that were carried away in the ship . . . ; others not knowing what should become of them and their little ones; others . . . melted in tears, seeing their poor little ones hanging about them, crying for fear and quaking with cold."[11]

Bradford and Brewster were among those left on the beach when the ship sailed away. They, along with all the others not on the Dutch vessel, were soon taken prisoner.

Once again, the authorities did not know what to do with the captured dissidents. For a while, they were moved from one jail to another. No one, though, seemed willing to keep the group—mostly women and children—in prison. Once again, they were eventually all released.

Meanwhile, the men on the ship might have been better off had they, too, been arrested. "[D]estitute . . . not having a cloth to shift them with . . . and some scarce a penny about them," they soon found themselves in the midst of a terrible storm that almost sent the Dutch ship to the bottom. In Bradford's words, "the water ran into their mouths and ears and the mariners cried out, 'We sink, we sink!'" Sailors and Saints alike raised their voices in prayer and, as if in answer to their prayers, "the ship not only did recover, but shortly after the . . . storm began to abate."[12] Still, it took fourteen days for them to sail the short distance between England and Holland.

After these two failed attempts to flee, the Separatists began to make their way across the North Sea singly or in small groups. Finally, by late 1608, "they all gat over . . . ," Bradford wrote, "and met together again according to their desires, with no small rejoicing."[13]

One of the last to arrive in Amsterdam was eighteen-year-old William Bradford. As he stepped off the ship that carried him to the great city of Amsterdam, he was still a minor character in the Pilgrim story. During the next dozen years in which he and the other Saints lived as exiles in a strange land, he moved closer to center stage as he prepared himself for the great adventure that awaited him in America.

THE PILGRIMS IN HOLLAND

"They knew they were pilgrims. . . ."[1]

Bradford and the other Saints from the villages around Scrooby must have been in awe when they saw Amsterdam for the first time. Crisscrossed by canals, with many houses built on stilts, the city was an architectural wonder and home to magnificent manors owned by prosperous merchants. No doubt Bradford and the others went sightseeing and were astonished by the luxurious, flower-filled gardens. They almost certainly visited the magnificent Royal Palace, built in 1565, and the famed *Oude Kirk*, or Old Church, already three hundred years old when the Saints made their way from England.

In the early seventeenth century, Holland was just beginning what is now considered its "Golden Age." After more than a century of domination by the Spanish, the Dutch had waged a terrible war to win their freedom. Having experienced persecution firsthand, they established what was then the most tolerant system of government in all Europe.

Under the rule of Prince William I, the Dutch people enjoyed freedom of religion as well as a degree of control over their political destinies that was unheard of in the rest of Europe. The Dutch also enjoyed freedom of the press at a time when scores of men languished in English prisons simply because they dared to write pamphlets or books that the English government or church found offensive.

At the same time, Holland was the world's leading center of trade and manufacturing. And the Dutch put the wealth they earned to good use. They built schools that were among the most advanced in Europe and homes and hospitals for the old and infirm. They were, by all accounts, kind, decent people. "They . . . will not Cozen [cheat] a Chylde or a stranger, in changing a peece of gold, nor in price or quality of things they buy," said an English tourist who visited Holland shortly before the Separatists arrived. "[T]hey love," he added, "equality in all things."[2]

As magnificent as the old city of Amsterdam was, however, and as kind and welcoming as most of the Dutch people were, the Separatists were not comfortable in their new home. They were, after all, surrounded by people speaking a language they didn't understand. Then, too, they had left their homes with little more than the clothes on their backs and now were unemployed. Most of them had been farmers. To survive in the bustling trading center of Amsterdam, they had to learn new trades. Bradford, in fact, soon apprenticed himself to a maker of silk. Others found similar, menial jobs. As Bradford later wrote, these jobs barely paid enough money for the Separatists to live. "[I]t was not long," he said, "before they saw the grim and grisly face of poverty coming upon them like an armed man."

This poverty, Bradford said, quickly became their greatest enemy, whom they knew they "must buckle and encounter, and from whom they could not fly."[3]

Even more serious problems stemmed from dissension within two other Separatist congregations that had preceded the Scrooby group to Holland. The Scrooby Separatists feared that this dissension could cause them problems with the Dutch authorities. And so, Bradford said, "They . . . thought it was best to remove before they were any way engaged [in those controversies]."[4] After just a year in Amsterdam, the Scrooby group moved again, to Leyden, a city about 25 miles (40 kilometers) away.

During the year Bradford lived in Amsterdam, he met Dorothy May, the girl he would eventually marry. Young "Dority," as she signed her name, must have been an attractive girl. Though she was just eleven years old when she and William met—probably at a church service—he immediately determined that she would someday be his wife. At that time, she was too young for him to court, even in those days when girls married while in their early teens. It appears, however, that Bradford and Dorothy's father reached an agreement sometime in 1609 that she would someday be William's bride.

William, then, had a special reason for feeling sad as he and the other Scrooby Separatists left Amsterdam. All in the group, however, were troubled as they got ready to move to a new city where they would have to start over. "[T]hey well knew," Bradford later said, "it would be much to the prejudice of their outward estates. . . ."[5] Still, they had no choice but to turn their backs on their troubled fellow Separatists in Amsterdam.

In the spring of 1609, Bradford and about one hundred others, including a number of discontented members of the other Amsterdam congregations, made their way to Leyden. Described by Bradford as "a fair and beautiful city and of a sweet situation,"[6] Leyden was one of the oldest and most famous cities in Holland.

Like Amsterdam, Leyden was a thriving city. It was the center of a flourishing cloth-making industry. Many of the new immigrants to the city found employment as apprentice weavers and ribbon and button makers. Bradford himself went to work as an apprentice maker of fustian, a cloth like corduroy. Eventually, he and the others were able to earn what Bradford called "a competent and comfortable living" but only by "hard and continual labor."[7]

The group lived near the center of the city, near St. Peter's Church, or *Pieterskerk*. The neighborhood in which they settled was one of the city's poorest, crowded with tiny apartments and homes built on narrow alleyways. On a narrow lane with the descriptive name of *Stinksteeg*, or Stink Alley, Bradford lived in a house with William Brewster and his family. Just a few doors away was a large dwelling that the group purchased to house John Robinson, who had been chosen the congregation's pastor. This substantial house also served as the group's meeting place.

During his first few years in Leyden, Bradford probably spent most of his time working hard just to survive. William's uncles died, and he inherited the Bradford family holdings in Yorkshire. In 1611, as soon as he came of age, he sold that property, including a house, cottage, and a small orchard, and used the profits from the sale to buy a small house not far from the university. At that time, he also set himself up in busi-

*The city of Leyden. One wonders if Bradford had
the time—or inclination—to take his future wife, Dority, for
a walk along the canal or out to see the windmills.*

ness, probably as a cloth-maker on a loom in his new home, and became a citizen of Leyden.

By late 1613, Bradford, now a property and business owner, was ready to marry sixteen-year-old Dorothy. On December 10, he and his bride were wed in Amsterdam.

We know almost nothing of the couple's years in Leyden beyond the fact that Dorothy gave birth to a son, John, sometime in 1615. Their days, though, must have been busy with work as William spent hours at his loom while Dorothy cared for little John as he toddled around the house. We do know there were many marriages in the Separatist community in those years, so it is likely the Bradfords socialized with those couples and their children. Bradford does give a hint that their lives were not all work. The Separatists, he said, enjoyed much "sweet and delightful society" in Leyden.[8]

Much of this socializing centered on church meetings. These meetings lasted almost all day each Sunday. At about eight o'clock in the morning, families filed into the large room on the first floor of John Robinson's large home.

Services started with about an hour of prayer. During this prayer, Bradford and the others stood by their seats, for the Separatists did not believe in kneeling or bowing like Catholics or Anglicans. After the prayer, Robinson read from the Bible and preached for two hours or more, with a couple of short breaks for the singing of psalms—without musical accompaniment. This sermonizing was followed by the celebration of the Lord's Supper and the taking of a collection. Finally, around midday, the congregation took another short break to eat and relax.

In the afternoon Robinson or perhaps Brewster, as the ruling elder, read a passage from the Bible, spoke about it briefly, and then opened the meeting for "prophesying." At this time any man in the group could speak about his own religious feelings and beliefs. This essentially democratic practice was one important way in which the Separatist services differed from those of the Puritans, where only preachers were allowed to speak.

During these years, the congregation grew until it had about three hundred members. Even as the group seemed to flourish, however, the Separatists were becoming unhappy in Holland. There were, Bradford later wrote, several reasons for this unhappiness.

For one thing, there was what he called the "hardness of the place and country"—the difficulties they faced in earning their livings. These conditions kept other dissidents in England from joining their group. So harsh were conditions, he said, that some who might have joined them "chose the prisons in England rather . . . than liberty in Holland with these afflictions." Others who did join were not able to "bide it out and continue with them."

The Separatists also saw that the hard work they had to do just to make ends meet was making them old before their time and, in Bradford's words, was making their children "decrepit in their early youth."

Even more troubling to Bradford and the others was that many of the children or younger members of the congregation were being seduced away from their faith by the fun-loving and easygoing Hollanders. "Some became soldiers, others took upon them[selves] far voyages by sea, and others some worse courses tending to . . . the danger of their souls," he wrote.[9]

At the same time, the Separatists were aware that a truce agreement that ended the fighting between the Netherlands and Spain in 1608 was set to expire in 1621. Thoughts of what might happen if war broke out again and Catholic Spain were to win and occupy Leyden filled the Separatists with unease.

By 1617 the Separatist leaders were talking about moving yet again. Motivated by what Bradford described as a "great hope or inward zeal" of establishing a settlement in some remote place where God's work could be done in peace, they were talking of leaving Holland and sailing across the ocean to the wilds of the Americas.[10]

By that time, Bradford was a successful man, a property owner, married, and a father. As Brewster's protégé, it would have been perfectly natural for him to be in a position of authority in the community of the Saints. As one of the group's leaders he certainly would have taken part in discussions about making a move from Holland to the Americas.

Meanwhile, though the Separatist leaders–presumably including Bradford–had decided that the group had no choice but to leave Holland, not all in the congregation were in agreement. For one thing, many did not want to leave the lifestyle they had built in Leyden to start over in an untamed land. Many were terrified at the prospect of a long and dangerous sea voyage, followed by even greater dangers in the wilderness.

Bradford and the other leaders calmed the fears of the would-be emigrants as best they could. "It was answered," Bradford later said, "that all great and honourable actions are accompanied with great difficulties and must be . . . overcome with answerable courages. . . . The difficulties were many, but not invincible."[11]

Deciding to move and actually moving were two different things, however. Transporting scores of people with their belongings and supplies, to start a settlement across the Atlantic Ocean was a huge undertaking. The Saints needed official approval to settle in their chosen destination of Virginia. They needed ships, and they needed a lot of money.

In early 1618 two deacons (elected nonclerical leaders) of the Leyden congregation–John Carver and Robert Cushman–were sent to England to obtain the legal documents and financial backing needed to transplant the group to the New World.

At that time, the settlement of Virginia was under the control of the Virginia Company of London. The members of this company had been granted a Royal Charter (something like a long-term lease) for the Virginia territory in exchange for their promise to support settlements in America. In turn, the company gave grants of land to groups of settlers who were willing to pay their own way to America.

During the next three years, Cushman and Carver were involved in almost constant negotiations with the Virginia Company and with the king's advisers. These negotiations seemed to drag on forever.

Finally, while James I would not give them a signed document promising them the freedom of religion they wanted, he did say he would "not molest them" in the New World, provided they "carried themselves peaceably."[12] Bradford reasoned that even the king's seal was no guarantee of safety. "If afterwards there should be a . . . desire to wrong them," Bradford said, "though they had a seal as broad as the house floor it would not [save them]."[13]

Meanwhile, as negotiations continued, Bradford and the others in Leyden received a letter from Cushman telling them of the fate of another group of Separatists whose ship had been blown off course when they tried to emigrate to Virginia in late 1618. As their vessel struggled westward, sickness broke out on board. The ship's captain, many crewmen, and scores of passengers died. "There are dead . . . 130 persons . . . it is said there was in all 180 persons in the ship, so as they were packed together like herrings," Cushman wrote.

". . . [I]t is . . . rather wondered at that so many are alive than that so many are dead."[14]

During this period, William Brewster made a journey to London to help Cushman and Carver in their negotiations. He was there, sometime in 1619, when a book he published critical of James I was brought to the attention of the king. Enraged, the king ordered Brewster arrested. Knowing his arrest would lead to his torture or execution, Brewster went into hiding. With his old friend and mentor unable to return to Holland and Cushman and Carver busy in London, it is likely that most of the responsibility of preparing for the departure of the congregation fell on William Bradford's shoulders.

Finally, in early 1620, the Virginia Company gave the Saints the document they wanted. Immediately, Cushman and Carver began trying to raise money to pay for the Saints' move to America. They were still looking for funds when they were approached by Thomas Weston, a London merchant who said that he and a group of his friends would "set them forth," supplying everything they needed to build a colony.[15] The colonists, for their part, would have to repay Weston and the other investors and provide them with profits.

Soon, articles of agreement forming a partnership between the Merchant Adventurers—as the investors were known—and the Planters—as those who would actually "plant" the settlement were called—were drawn up and approved by both sides. This agreement required the Adventurers to provide ships and supplies to the Saints in exchange for seven years of work. During that time any money the Saints earned as fishermen and farmers would go to pay the debt owed to the Adventurers. Once that debt was paid, all profits would be held as "common stock" (in something like an escrow account) until the end of the seven-year period, when profits would be divided between the Planters and the Adventurers. The agreement also allowed the settlers to work two days each week for their own benefit and stated that at the end of the seven-year partnership, the Planters would own their own homes and lands in the New World.

Soon after, however, Weston wrote from London changing the contract. His new terms called for the land cleared by the Saints and the homes they built to be placed in common stock at the end of the partnership and then divided among the Adventurers and Planters. The new contract also required the settlers to work only for the common good. The Saints hated these new terms, which were almost the same as if they were signing on as indentured servants.

Cushman, in England, agreed to the new terms without bothering to consult with Bradford and the others still in Holland. In his defense, Cushman realized that the Saints had no choice. They had already sold their homes and invested what little money they had in the colonial venture. It was either accept what Weston offered or stay in Leyden, penniless and homeless.

Many in the congregation who had planned to emigrate did just that, preferring poverty in Holland to what they viewed as servitude in the New World. Suddenly it became clear to Weston and the other Adventurers that there were not enough Saints willing to emigrate to make the colony a success. Quickly, they recruited about sixty settlers from London and the surrounding countryside. These recruits were enlisted willy-nilly, without any regard to their religious beliefs or, for that matter, their backgrounds. They were, in a real sense, no more than "warm bodies" needed to people a new settlement. Known by the Saints as "Strangers," many of these non-Separatists proved to be valuable members of the little community that would ultimately be founded in Massachusetts. Others proved to be nothing but trouble.

Finally, by mid-1620, plans for departure started moving rapidly. The Leyden group—chiefly Bradford—purchased a small ship called the *Speedwell*, not much larger than a modern cruising sailboat. In England, at the same time, the Weston group chartered a larger ship. This vessel was the *Mayflower*.

Plans called for the *Speedwell* to carry the Separatists to England, where they would join the other settlers and the *Mayflower*. The two vessels would then sail together across the Atlantic to America. The *Mayflower* would return to England, and the *Speedwell* would remain with the settlers, where they could use her as a fishing vessel.

In late July 1620 about fifty Separatist men, women, and children departed from Leyden. Traveling on canalboats, they made their way to the port city of Delftshaven. Bradford, in his history, wrote many years later of their departure.

"And the time being come that they must depart," he said, "they were accompanied with most of their brethren out of the city unto a town . . . where the ship lay ready to receive them. So they left the goodly and pleasant city which had been their resting place near twelve years. . . ." As they departed from Leyden, he added, ". . . they knew they were pilgrims. . . ."[16]

In that phrase, written in his journal a decade after leaving Leyden, William Bradford gave the Pilgrims their name. And though the people we know today as Pilgrims never used that name to describe themselves, they were, indeed, pilgrims. They were wanderers–men, women, and children journeying in search of freedom and willing to risk danger and death in the name of their beliefs.

4

Trials at Sea

"After long beating at sea they fell with that land which is called Cape Cod; the which being made and certainly known to be it, they were not a little joyful."[1]

On July 21, 1620, Bradford and the others bound for America reached the port city of Delftshaven just a few miles south of Rotterdam. There they found the *Speedwell* moored at the city quay. Many of the Saints must have been stunned when they first saw the little ship, for she was only about 50 feet (15 meters) long. Perhaps Bradford–who, we may assume, had read John Smith's account of the settlement of Jamestown–calmed their fears by reminding them that the *Discovery* and the *Godspeed*, two of the ships that carried the first colonists safely to Virginia, had been even smaller.

In any event, after spending the night in the city, Bradford and the other Pilgrims boarded the little ship. Friends and loved ones clambered on board to embrace and kiss those who were leaving on the dangerous voyage to England and then on to the New World.

According to Bradford, "tears did gush from every eye" as the Pilgrims bade good-bye to friends and relatives.[2] There was good reason for tears. Except for Pastor Robinson, all the church leaders were leaving. About a half-dozen families were being separated, including the Bradford family, for William and Dorothy were leaving five-year-old John behind, probably in Pastor Robinson's care.

The Brewster family, as well, was being split as Mary, Brewster's wife, climbed on board the *Speedwell* with the couple's two youngest sons, Wrestling (for "wrestling" with Satan) and Love, while their eldest son, Jonathan, and their two youngest daughters, Fear and Patience, remained in Holland. Though all those families hoped they would soon be reunited, all feared they would never see their loved ones again. In many cases, those fears were justified.

Meanwhile, the Pilgrims on the *Speedwell* were an unlikely group to be setting out to build a settlement. Of the forty-six Saints leaving Holland, nineteen were children and eleven were women. Just sixteen in the group were grown men. No other attempt to found a settlement in America had included so many women and children, or so few adult males.

It was a heartbreaking scene as these men, women, and children crowded along the little ship's rails waving farewell to friends and loved ones, while the *Speedwell*'s crew carefully worked the vessel from dockside and then down a narrow inlet toward the open ocean. William and Dorothy almost certainly stood side by side, both weeping, as they strained to catch a final glimpse of John.

Soon, however, Delftshaven slipped astern and the *Speedwell* entered the open waters of the North Sea, headed southwest toward the coast of England. Pushed by what Bradford later described as a "prosperous wind,"[3] the vessel made good time on her crossing to the harbor of Southampton on England's south coast. There, Bradford and the others found the *Mayflower* waiting with the so-called Strangers chosen by Weston to help settle the new colony already on board.

In Southampton, Bradford also found his old friend Brewster, hiding below deck on the *Mayflower*. Still wanted by the authorities, he had sneaked on board when the ship was in London. On her passenger list he was recorded as "Mr. Williamson," a name chosen, no doubt, because his father's name, like his, was William. The reunion of the two friends must have been joyous as they brought each other up to date on all that had happened in England and in Leyden and discussed what might lie ahead in America.

Even in Southampton, on the eve of their departure for America, the Saints and their financial backers continued bickering. By this time, the Saints were insisting they would never sign the new contract that had been presented by Weston and the other investors. Angry, Weston told them they would either sign or receive no more financial help from the Adventurers. Still refusing to sign, the Saints had to sell some of their own supplies—about two tons of butter—to raise money they needed to clear port.

Finally, on August 5, without ever having signed Weston's partnership agreement, the Saints and Strangers set sail from Southampton. Because Weston had refused to advance them any more funds, they sailed "scarce having any butter, no oil, not a sole to mend a shoe, nor every man a sword to his side, wanteing many muskets, much armor, etc. . . ."[4]

As the two ships left Southampton the *Mayflower* led the way, followed by the *Speedwell*. About ninety passengers were on board the *Mayflower*, and thirty or so–including Bradford, Brewster, and the other Separatist leaders–on board the smaller vessel.

The two ships were still within sight of land when the captain of the *Speedwell*, a man named Reynolds, signaled that the ship was leaking badly. The ships turned back, docking in Dartmouth, between Southampton and the open ocean.

In port, the *Speedwell* was checked from stem to stern, but no reason could be found that would explain why she leaked so badly when under way. After a delay of about two weeks, the two vessels set sail again. This time, they had sailed about 300 miles (480 kilometers) when Reynolds signaled that the *Speedwell* again was in difficulty.

Once more, the two ships returned to England, where they dropped their anchors in the port of Plymouth. According to Robert Cushman, one of the passengers on board the smaller vessel, they made it back just in time. "If we had stayed at sea but three or four hours more, she would have sunk right down. . . . [S]he is as open and leaky as a sieve," Cushman wrote in a letter to a friend. "[I]f ever we make a plantation (a colony)," he added, "God works a miracle."[5]

While Cushman's pessimism stemmed at least in part from the fact that he had been violently seasick all the time he was on board the *Speedwell*, he was right about one thing: The *Speedwell* was in no condition to make an ocean crossing. The Pilgrims had no choice but to abandon the ship in Plymouth.

Having to leave the small ship behind in England was a bitter blow. It meant that the Pilgrims would not

The Mayflower *under sail.*

be able to use her as a fishing vessel and coastal trader, as they had planned, and that they would lose their main means of supporting themselves in America. Worse, with the *Speedwell* gone, the number of settlers would have to be reduced, for there was no way that one hundred and twenty passengers would fit on the tiny *Mayflower*.

As it turned out, there was no shortage of volunteers to stay behind and wait for a later ship. All the troubles aboard the *Speedwell* apparently convinced some in the group that the voyage might be doomed.

Finally, on September 6, the *Mayflower* departed from Plymouth. All told, there were one hundred and two passengers on board the vessel as she wallowed her way from Plymouth into the open ocean. Contrary to myth, these passengers were anything but a unified group of dissidents looking for religious freedom in America. In fact, sixty of the passengers were non-Separatists. This number included forty-two Strangers recruited by Weston and his friends, and about eighteen indentured servants and hired men. While some of these non-Separatists were Puritans, most were Anglicans. Just forty-two of the passengers were Saints. Of that number, only Bradford, Brewster, and Brewster's wife, Mary, had been members of the original Scrooby congregation. Most of the remaining Saints had joined the Leyden congregation in Holland, while a small number had been recruited in England.

If there was one characteristic that was shared by all the Pilgrims–a name usually used to describe all who sailed on the *Mayflower*, Saint and Stranger alike–it was that virtually all were ordinary men and women. They were farmers and tradesmen and craftsmen and more than a few unemployed men who had been recruited from London's poorest neighborhoods. None were highborn. None had titles or coats of arms. These settlers were from England's cottages and farms, not her manor houses and castles.

Another popular misconception is that the Pilgrims were old. The truth is that about one-third of the *Mayflower*'s passengers were children under the age of fifteen. The great majority of the adult male passengers were not the dusty graybeards usually portrayed in pictures of the Pilgrim Fathers. They were in their twenties. In fact, only seven were aged forty or older. Of the women, only one, Mary Brewster, was over the age of forty.

With all these men, women, and children on board, the *Mayflower* was overcrowded. Only Captain Jones enjoyed his own space on board, and even his cabin, perched in the "sterncastle" below the aft, or poop, deck, was about the size of a small walk-in closet. Thirty or so crewmen shared quarters in a small cabin far forward, in what was known as the forecastle (pronounced "fo'c's'le" with all the syllables run together). All the passengers were housed in what might be called the main cabin—a tiny space about 20 feet (6 meters) square in the ship's stern—and in what was known as the "'tween decks," the space between the main deck and the cargo hold below.

To get an idea of how crowded it was, try to imagine one hundred men, women, and children living day after day, sleeping and eating and doing all the other things that people do every day and night in a space about the size of a one-bedroom apartment.

Fortunately, the *Mayflower* for years had been used to haul cloth and dry-goods from England to France, returning with casks of wine and spirits. That meant she was a "sweet" ship, that she didn't stink as she would have if she had been used to haul fish or some other foul-smelling cargo. Still, the passengers were miserable. Soon after leaving Plymouth the ship entered the open ocean, where she pitched and yawed her way from wave to wave so that, "many were afflicted with sea-sickness."[6] There were no toilet facilities on board. The brave or desperate could perch on a platform beneath the bow sprit (in what was known as the ship's "heads") to relieve themselves or use a wooden bucket with little or no privacy. There were no provisions for bathing or washing clothes. As you might imagine, the stench below deck was terrible.

As the ship plowed her way westward at a top speed of about 7 miles (11 kilometers) per hour, the tedium on board was like torture. The Pilgrims were soon afflicted by boils caused by living in constant dampness. The slightest movements as the ship rolled her way from wave to wave caused pain. Meals offered no relief since they were, for the most part, eaten cold and consisted only of hard, weevil-infested biscuits, moldy cheese, and salted fish or dried pork or beef (called "salt horse" by the sailors) washed down by beer.

Somehow, with all the filth and vermin that infested their quarters, the Pilgrims managed to avoid serious illness. In fact, only one passenger died during the voyage. That was remarkable since it was common for vessels in those days to be swept by deadly diseases including scurvy (caused by a vitamin C deficiency), smallpox, and dysentery as they made ocean passages.

The only other fatality during the voyage was a member of the crew–a young man who had taunted the Pilgrims and laughed as he said he looked forward to burying them at sea. Instead, he himself fell ill–probably with dysentery–and died. Bradford, not surprisingly given his religious beliefs, viewed the young sailor's death as punishment handed out by Divine Providence.

For a time, Bradford later wrote, they "enjoyed fair winds and weather." Then, after they had passed the midpoint in their voyage, the weather changed and they "met with many fierce storms with which the ship was [wickedly] shaken."[7]

When the storms struck, the landlubbers on the *Mayflower* must have thought they were trapped in a nightmare. The wind screamed in the ship's rigging. Tons of blue-black water crashed down on her decks as she pitched and rolled at the mercy of huge waves. Belowdecks the passengers, already weakened by seasickness, by weeks without fresh air, good food, and exercise, their legs rubbery with fear, whimpered or screamed or prayed as icy water cascaded below through deck boards loosened by the pounding of the seas.

In the midst of this terror, a thick oak beam supporting the vessel's main deck cracked with a sound like a musket shot. Seawater poured into the 'tween-deck cabin as Saints and Strangers alike prayed for deliverance. Suddenly, one of the Leyden group remembered that they had brought on board what Bradford described as a "large screw"—something like a car jack—that could be used to repair the broken beam. With the storm still raging, the repair was made.

By that time many of the passengers and even some of the mariners on board wanted to turn back. Captain Jones, though, was not ready to give up. He was convinced his ship was sound, that she would ride out the storm. "So," Bradford said, "they committed themselves to the will of God and resolved to proceed."[8]

As they pressed on, the storms grew worse. Jones, employing all his old salt's knowledge, ordered the *Mayflower*'s sails struck so she could sail under what mariners called "bare poles." For days the ship drifted at the mercy of the wind and waves like a piece of flotsam. For hour after hour she was rolled from side to side. Seas taller than her mast tops threatened to send her to the bottom.

In this period one of the passengers, a servant named John Howland, made his way to the deck to steal a breath of fresh air. "With a [pitch] of the ship," Bradford later wrote, "[he was] thrown into the sea. . . ." Somehow, Howland managed to grab a line trailing from the vessel's mainmast. Though he was carried deep beneath the waves, he held on until, in Bradford's words, "he was hauled up . . . and then with a boat hook and other means got into the ship again." Howland survived and, in fact, lived to be an old-timer who undoubtedly spent hours telling his grandchildren the story of his miraculous escape.[9]

In the midst of the storms, as the ship was hurled from wave to wave, Elizabeth Hopkins, one of the Saints, gave birth to a son. Fittingly enough, the baby was named Oceanus.

Finally, the storms began to weaken. The friendly weather was gone, however, and for the balance of the voyage Captain Jones and his crew had to work hard sailing against the prevailing winds. Finally, at daybreak on November 9, 1620, after what Bradford described as a "long beating at sea," those on the *Mayflower* spied the highlands of Cape Cod. All on board, Bradford wrote about ten years later, were "not a little joyful."[10]

If he and the other Pilgrims had any idea what lay in store for them, they would have not been so happy. For William Bradford and the Pilgrims of Plymouth Colony were about to face trials and difficulties they could not even imagine.

≈ 5 ≈

THE MAYFLOWER COMPACT

"[It] was thought good there should be an association and agreement that we should combine together in one body, and to submit to such . . . governors as we should by common consent agree to make and choose. . . ."
Mourt's Relation[1]

On a map, Cape Cod looks like a bent arm extending about 30 miles (48 kilometers) east from the coast of Massachusetts before turning to run in a northerly direction for another 30 miles or so. The cape was named by an English seaman, Captain Bartholomew Gosnold, who visited New England in 1602 and discovered its waters teeming with fat codfish. Gosnold had come to the coast in search of sassafras root, then considered a medicine that cured "large importunate fevers . . . griefes of the breast caused of cold humors, [and] griefes of the heade" while bringing relief to "them that bee lame and creeples [cripples] and them that are not able to goe."[2] He and his men went ashore on the cape, marking the first known landing of a European in Massachusetts. They gathered firewood and sassafras roots, then reboarded their vessel to sail south along the coast until they entered an area filled with rocks and shoals. The men on Gosnold's vessel named this spot Tucker's Terror, presumably in memory of one of their mates who must have panicked at the sight of roaring breakers all around their ship.

When William Bradford and the others on the *Mayflower* spied the cape on November 9, 1620, they must have wanted desperately to escape from the crowded, dirty, uncomfortable vessel that had been their home for sixty-four days. Instead of making for land, however, Captain Jones ordered the ship turned south, toward the northern reaches of the Virginia Colony, where the Pilgrims had been directed to plant their settlement.

All day on November 9 the *Mayflower* sailed in Bartholomew Gosnold's wake. Jones, a canny ship master, had lookouts high in the vessel's mast tops, their eyes peeled for danger. As the sun slid toward the western horizon, the ship, in Bradford's words, "fell amongst dangerous shoals and roaring breakers. . . ." Despite her master's care, the vessel had sailed into the midst of Tucker's Terror.[3]

With the sky starting to darken and the wind dropping as it almost always does at nightfall, those on the ship "conceived themselves in great danger," Bradford said.[4] After consulting with the Pilgrim leaders, Jones decided to turn his ship north and anchor in an open bay that he knew lay behind Cape Cod. Carefully, he conned the *Mayflower* through the shoal waters until she was free of danger and sailing north again.

Some historians claim that the Pilgrims never intended to settle in the Virginia Colony; that they always planned to plant their colony in New England. The best evidence, however, that they intended to follow the instructions in their patent is this nearly disastrous attempt to sail down the coast of Cape Cod. Why else would the weary men and women on the *Mayflower*–including Jones and his crew–have bothered sailing south at all if not to go to Virginia? At the same time, the story that they were turned back by the deadly rocks and shoals of Tucker's Terror (now known as Pollock Rip) makes perfect sense. "No sailor who has weathered Cape Cod needs any better explanation than . . . Pollock Rip to explain why the *Mayflower* turned back," said the historian Samuel Eliot Morison, a famous sailor in his own right, in writing about the *Mayflower*'s voyage.[5]

In any event, by nightfall on November 10 the ship was once again at the north end of the cape. All that night the *Mayflower* tacked back and forth a few miles offshore. At sunrise the next morning, Jones ordered her course changed. Slowly, the vessel entered Cape Cod Bay.

Since none on board the ship ever described in any detail what it was like on the ship that morning, we don't know for sure. But it isn't hard to imagine the *Mayflower*, with her canvas and rigging tattered and her topsides white with salt spray, inching her way forward in the early morning light as seagulls wheeled and cawed over the heads of the sailors who had climbed her rigging to get ready to strike her sails.

As the ship moved slowly into the bay, a deckhand near the bow heaved a lead-weighted line into the dark waters again and again, measuring the water's depth by counting knots or other "marks" placed every fathom, or 6 feet (2 meters), along the length of the line. Jones, at his post on the poop deck, listened carefully to this leadsman's chanting calls. "By the mark, ten, sir!" let the captain know the water was 60 feet (18 meters) deep. Then, "By the mark, eight, sir!" And finally, "By the mark, five, sir!" meaning the water was five fathoms, or 30 feet (9 meters), deep. At that cry, Jones knew it was time to anchor.

At the captain's order, sailors aloft struck the ship's sails while the helmsman turned her bow into the wind. In moments, the *Mayflower* drifted to a stop and began moving backward. Deckhands let the ship's heavy anchor go. With a clanking rattle of its chain, the anchor plunged down until its flukes bit into the bottom of the bay and the *Mayflower* came to rest. In Bradford's words, "they rid in safety."[6]

As the *Mayflower* rocked at anchor in the large bay that nestles between Cape Cod and the mainland coast of Massachusetts, Bradford, Dorothy, and other passengers undoubtedly crowded the rails while the more adventuresome children clambered up the ratlines like monkeys. What they saw was both beautiful and forbidding: an empty beach bordered by a wild, untamed forest of juniper and pine and oak trees. Someone—perhaps Bradford himself or Brewster—suggested that they offer a prayer of thanks, and, Bradford said, they fell to their knees on the ship's wooden deck and "blessed the God of Heaven who had brought them over the vast and furious ocean, and delivered them from all the perils and miseries therof, again to set their feet on the firm and stable earth. . . ."[7]

Although the passengers and crew on board must have been eager to get ashore, to once again feel terra firma beneath their feet, Bradford and the other Pilgrim leaders soon let them know there would be no landing just yet. There was business that had to be tended to before any could set foot on American soil.

Just one day earlier, as the *Mayflower* made her way from Tucker's Terror to the north end of Cape Cod, some of the Strangers on board had started grumbling. If the ship put them ashore outside the boundaries of the original patent, these Strangers muttered, no one on board would have the right to tell them how to act or what to do. Hearing these "discontented and mutinous speeches,"[8] Bradford and the other leaders knew they had to take action. If they didn't–if the passengers divided into two groups–there would be a good chance that all, Saint and Stranger alike, would die in the wilderness.

At this time, Bradford surely remembered Pastor John Robinson's advice, given to all the Saints in a letter before they departed from Holland. Robinson had warned them to beware of dissension as they tried to establish their settlement: "[A]s men are careful not to have a new house shaken with any violence before it be well settled and the parts firmly knit, so be you . . . much more careful that the house of God, which you are and are to be, be not shaken with . . . oppositions at the first settling therof." To keep the colony safe and whole, they should create "a body politic," a civil government, "not furnished with any persons of special eminency above the rest, to be chosen by you into office. . . ." What better time than now, when faced with dissension, Bradford and the others reasoned, to form that "body politic"?[9]

With that in mind, the Pilgrim leaders wrote what Bradford called "the first foundation of their government."[10] Though we don't know for sure who wrote what has come to be known as the Mayflower Compact, it is apparent from its legal language that William Brewster– a former civil servant–must have had a hand in it. And

it makes sense that if Brewster was one of the writers of
the compact, then his friend and protégé Bradford had
a hand in it as well.

> *In the name of God, Amen. We whose names
> are underwritten . . . do by these presents sol-
> emnly and mutually in the presence of God and
> of one another, covenant and combine ourselves
> together into a civil body politic . . . and . . .
> hereof to enact, constitute, and frame such just
> and equal laws, ordinances, acts, constitutions,
> offices, from time to time, as shall be thought most
> meet and convenient for the general good of the
> colony: unto which we promise all due submission
> and obedience. . . .*[11]

The compact was signed by every adult male passenger on the *Mayflower* except for two hired men who
had no intention of becoming a permanent part of the
colony. John Carver, the Saint who had worked tire-
lessly to obtain the Pilgrims' patent, was the first to sign.
Bradford wrote his name below Carver's. Brewster
signed next, then the rest of the Pilgrims.

Today, the agreement signed by the Saints and
Strangers on board the *Mayflower* is as famous as the
Pilgrims themselves. The compact, however, was not
as has sometimes been claimed, the cornerstone of
the American system of democracy. For one thing, it
did not guarantee equal treatment to all colonists and
gave no rights to women, who were considered "chat-
tel"–the property of their husbands. It is not realistic
for us to think that the simple farmers and craftsmen
on board the *Mayflower* could conceive of making the
giant leap from the feudal system they knew in En-

gland to the full-fledged system of democracy we know in America.

For its time, however, the compact was a remarkable document. It established a system of local self-government. It gave the Pilgrims of Plymouth a government "of the people," or at least the free, male people, to a degree that was unheard of in Europe. John Quincy Adams, the sixth president of the United States, called it the "first example in modern times of a . . . system of government instituted by voluntary agreement . . . by men of equal rights and about to establish their community in a new country."[12] In fact, for all its shortcomings, the Mayflower Compact was the first faltering step along a historical path that eventually led to the Declaration of Independence and the Constitution.

Soon after signing the compact, those who signed elected John Carver the first governor of Plymouth Plantation. In its own way, the election of Carver—a wealthy, fifty-four-year-old merchant who had been one of the Leyden group's leaders for several years—was every bit as important as the signing of the Mayflower Compact. The vote on the *Mayflower* as she lay at anchor off Cape Cod marked the first time that a New World colonial governor was democratically elected by a vote of the individuals governed.

Finally, with what might have proved to be a troublesome rift between the Saints and Strangers seemingly healed and the colony's leadership established, William Bradford and the other Pilgrims were ready to go ashore.

❧ 6 ❧

THE FIRST DISCOVERIES

"[S]o soon as we could we set ashore ... men, well armed, with some to fetch wood, for we had none left, as also to see what the land was, and what inhabitants they could meet with."[1]

Almost immediately after the signing of the Mayflower Compact a group of about sixteen Pilgrim men—including William Bradford—volunteered to go ashore under the command of Captain Myles (also spelled Miles) Standish, a thirty-six-year-old soldier of fortune who had been hired by the Pilgrims to serve as their military commander.

This soldier-for-hire became one of the most famous of all the Pilgrims because of a poem, *The Courtship of Myles Standish*, written in the mid-1800s by Henry Wadsworth Longfellow. That poem also brought fame to John Alden, a Stranger hired by the Pilgrims as a carpenter and barrel maker, and to Priscilla Mullins, a teenaged Pilgrim maid who was, according to Longfellow, loved by both Alden and Standish. While

Longfellow's poem makes for enjoyable reading, it is historically inaccurate. As so often happened with the Pilgrims, however, myth—or, in this case, poetry—came to be believed as the truth.

The truth is that Standish was an able military man who had, it is thought, served as a mercenary soldier in the war between the Spanish and Dutch for control of the Netherlands. As such, he was a natural choice to lead the Pilgrims on their first exploring party ashore. Indeed, Bradford and the others who volunteered to go exploring on November 11 were undoubtedly pleased to have a professional soldier as their leader. For all they knew, as soon as they stepped ashore they might well be attacked by Indians or by ravenous beasts, including lions, which some believed lurked in the woods of America.

It must have been late in the day when the volunteers climbed into the ship's longboat. With their muskets at the ready, armed with cutlasses and protected by armor helmets and breastplates called corselets, they set out for the beach with members of the ship's crew laboring at the oars.

That first day the explorers stayed on shore only long enough to get an idea of the lay of the land. They marched across the northern end of Cape Cod until they saw the Atlantic stretching to the eastern horizon. They explored a bit without finding any sign of Indians or ravenous beasts and then returned to the ship, carrying armloads of juniper to burn in the galley so the "sweet and strong" wood smoke would mask the stench in the crowded belowdecks area.[2]

Two days later, all the passengers who were not too weak from scurvy or simply worn out by the ocean voyage seem to have made it ashore. There the men

An artist's rendition of the signing of the Mayflower Compact.

and older boys explored and searched for food while the children, cooped up for weeks, played in the surf or chased seagulls along the beach. The women–as women did on Mondays in New England for generations–washed clothes.

Someone, perhaps one of the children, discovered the shallows were thick with clams and mussels. Starved for food other than the moldy cheese, salt horse, and hard biscuits they had been forced to eat for weeks at sea, the Pilgrims celebrated with a New England clambake. Not surprisingly, this sudden change in their diet made more than half the Pilgrims and many of the sailors "cast and scour"[3]–Bradford's way of saying they suffered diarrhea and vomiting.

Some of the signatures on the Mayflower Compact.

Sickness from a change in diet, though, was the least of the Pilgrims' problems. Bradford later wrote about those days:

> *I cannot but . . . stand half amazed at this poor people's . . . condition. Being thus passed the vast ocean, and a sea of troubles . . . they had now . . . no houses . . . to repair to. . . . And for the season, it was winter, and they [knew] . . . the winters of that country . . . to be sharp and violent, and subject to cruel and fierce storms, dangerous to travel to known places, much more to search an unknown coast. Besides, what could they see but a hideous and desolate wilderness, full of wild*

beasts and wild men. . . . If they looked behind them, there was the mighty ocean which they had passed and was now as a main bar and gulf to separate them from all the civil parts of the world.[4]

Anxious to secure housing on shore, the Pilgrim men made several more visits to the shore. They had planned to sail along the coast in a shallop (a large boat that can be either rowed or sailed) that had been carried in pieces from England on the *Mayflower*. Unfortunately, the shallop was, in Bradford's words, "bruised and shattered" from the beating it sustained during the ocean crossing.[5] As a consequence, while the ship's carpenters worked to repair the shallop, the Pilgrims were forced to explore on foot.

On November 15, Standish again led a party of men to the shore. The men formed a single-file line and headed along the beach. A spaniel, one of two dogs that made the voyage from England, played at their heels as they trudged along just above the high-water mark. Suddenly, they saw five or six Indians with a dog of their own heading in their direction. As soon as the Indians spied the Pilgrims, they scampered into the woods bordering the beach. The Indians' dog must have wanted to make friends with the Pilgrims' spaniel, for it refused to run until its masters "whistled [it] after them."[6]

Standish, Bradford, and the others pursued the Indians partly, Bradford said, "to see if they could speak to them" and partly to learn how many warriors were nearby.[7] Weighed down with their weapons and armor, however, and weakened by their long sea voyage, the Englishmen had no hope of catching the Indians.

In fact, the Pilgrims were probably lucky they didn't catch the Native Americans, who were members of the Pamet tribe. Though the Pamets were peaceful hunters, they would have been ready to fight if they felt threatened by the Englishmen. And if there had been a battle, the Pamets–who vastly outnumbered the explorers–almost certainly would have captured or killed the Pilgrims.

The Pilgrims followed the Indians for about 2 miles (3 kilometers) to a beach on the Atlantic side of Cape Cod. By that time it was near sunset, and the Pilgrims were exhausted and cold from slogging through the sand in their heavy armor. They made camp, set out sentinels, and, in the words of Bradford, "rested in quiet that night."[8]

The next day, the Pilgrims again tried to make contact with the Pamets. Again, they had no luck. All their marching and searching was difficult work, and they were, Bradford said, "distressed for want of drink." Soon, however, they stumbled across a pond where they "refreshed themselves, being the first New England water they drunk of. . . . " The water, he added, "was . . . as pleasant unto them as wine or beer had been in foretimes."[9]

That was quite a compliment since the typical English man or woman in the early 1600s thought water was downright bad for the health and–unlike the Puritans who frowned on drinking–dearly loved beer, wine, and other spirits, which they regarded as essential parts of any well-balanced diet.

Having "refreshed themselves," the Pilgrims set out again, moving down the center of the cape until they reached what is now the Little Pamet River. Along the way, they found another freshwater pond near what is today the town of Truro. They also came across several mounds of sand. Digging into one of these they unearthed a bow and some arrows that fell apart as they were handled. Convinced that they had opened an Indian grave, they quickly, in Bradford's words, "put in the bow again and made it up as it was, and left the rest untouched, because we thought it would be odious unto them to ransack their sepulchres."[10]

Not far from the grave, they found several patches of cleared land, the remains of a house, a large iron kettle, and another mound. This mound was larger than the grave they had opened and was different, Bradford said, in that it "was newly done, [so] we might see how they had paddled it with their hands. . . . "

Posting guards, Bradford and the others dug into the mound. In minutes, they uncovered several baskets, full of what Bradford called "very fair corn, with some thirty-six goodly ears of corn, some yellow, and some red, and others mixed with blue." It was, he added, "a very goodly sight." In honor of their discovery, the Pilgrims named the spot Corn Hill, a name it still bears today.[11]

Indeed, Bradford and the others knew that the corn they had just found could make the difference between survival and starvation. Though the Pilgrims had brought seed with them—including barley, wheat, and peas—they knew from Captain John Smith's writings that the best crop in America was corn. Now they had a supply of seed, theirs for the taking. And take it they did, packing as much as they could into the iron kettle they had found and filling their pockets with loose kernels.

Of course, what the Pilgrims did was stealing. And the theft was serious, since the Indians who had buried the corn would need it for planting in the spring if they were to avoid starvation themselves. Bradford and the others, however, promised themselves that they would return when their shallop was repaired to, in Bradford's words, "give them the kettle again, and satisfy them for their corn."[12]

The night of November 17, Bradford and his companions again camped out in the open. The next morning, as they made their way back across the cape, they got lost in the woods. While lost they came across what Bradford described as "a tree, where a young [sapling] was bowed down . . . , and some acorns strewed underneath."[13] Stephen Hopkins, one of the Strangers who earlier had spent time in Virginia, said it was an Indian deer snare. Bradford, curious, was investigating the trap when he somehow set it off and was left hanging by one leg while the other men in the party undoubtedly roared with laughter. He was cut free, and the party made their way back to the ship.

We can be sure those on the *Mayflower* gathered around the explorers as soon as they clambered on board. It is easy to imagine the questions and the gasps of wonder as Bradford and the others talked about the Indians they had seen. It is just as easy to imagine the laughter at Bradford's expense when the explorers told how he had been snatched into the air by the Indian trap. There must have been prayers of thanks when they showed the corn they had carried on board, for these farm folk knew those red, yellow, and blue kernels were a sign they might expect bountiful crops in the seasons ahead. The Pilgrims, Bradford said, "were marvelously glad and their hearts encouraged."[14]

In the days that followed this first exploration of Cape Cod, Bradford and the others made several more visits to explore further and to work on the shallop that had been dragged ashore. On each visit those who went ashore had to wade from the longboat to the beach. The cold water, Bradford later wrote, ". . . caused many to get colds and coughs, for it was nigh times freezing cold weather."[15] Though they were confined to their quarters, probably with pneumonia, the sickness also infected many of the *Mayflower*'s officers and crew. By late November the Pilgrims knew they had to act quickly to find a suitable place to build shelters or all might die.

Finally, on November 27, the ship's carpenter said the shallop was ready to sail. At last the Pilgrims would be able to explore in earnest, to find a spot to build their homes, to get all the weak and sick off the cramped and uncomfortable *Mayflower* and safe on land.

PLYMOUTH

"We marched . . . into the land, and found diverse
cornfields, and little running brooks, a place very
good for situation, so we returned to our ship
again and with good news to the rest of our people,
which did much comfort their hearts."[1]

By late November, when the shallop was finally sea-
worthy, there was an undeniable sense of urgency about
the Pilgrims' attempts to find a place to settle. The New
England winter was upon them with its cold winds, icy
rains, and snow; and the food supplies on the *Mayflower*
were running dangerously low.

On November 28, two dozen Pilgrims, including
William Bradford, set out with ten sailors in the shallop
to investigate the area to the south of their anchorage,
near the spot they had named Corn Hill. This large
group of explorers was led by the *Mayflower*'s master,
Christopher Jones, put in command by the Pilgrims to
repay him for what Bradford called his "kindness and
forwardness."[2]

Soon after the explorers set out in the shallop, the weather turned foul. The little vessel–only about 40 feet (12 meters) long and open to the weather–was forced to anchor in the lee of the cape, protected from high winds and wild waves. After an uncomfortable night in which "it blowed and did snow . . . and froze withal . . . ," the explorers made their way to the mouth of the Pamet River, which they named Cold Harbor for obvious reasons. All that day, they marched along the river's banks, up and down snow-covered hills, as the shallop followed in the river. Finally, exhausted, they made camp in a stand of pine trees. That night, thanks to some good shooting by someone in the group, they dined on "three fat geese and six ducks" with what Bradford called "soldiers' stomachs."[3]

The next morning, the explorers trekked the few miles north to Corn Hill, where they dug up about a dozen more bushels of corn. These were sent back by shallop to the *Mayflower* as Bradford and others continued to explore.

After another night spent in the open, the explorers followed "paths and tracks of the Indians" into the woods, hoping the forest trails would lead them to "some town, or houses."[4] Finally, giving up the hunt, they were on their way back to the beach when they stumbled across a large earthen mound, in which they found "bowls, trays, dishes, and such like trinkets." They also uncovered the remains of a light-haired man, probably a European sailor, and the skeleton of a small child. Though the Pilgrims had been careful not to disturb any of the Indian graves, they had no qualms about stealing from the grave of this supposed European. "We brought," Bradford said, "sundry of the prettiest things away with us, and covered the corpse up again."[5]

Later that same day, they discovered a pair of Indian dwellings. "The houses," Bradford said, "were made with long young sapling trees, bended and both ends stuck into the ground." Round and covered with thick mats, they were large enough for a man to stand upright. Whoever had lived in them must have departed quickly, for they left behind bowls, trays, earthen pots, baskets made of crab shells, "and sundry other of their household stuff."

The Pilgrims carried away what Bradford called "some of the best things" they found in the dwellings. Once again, as they had in the past, they promised themselves they would return with beads and other items to prove they wanted to "truck (trade) with them" and not steal.[6]

Back on board the *Mayflower*, lively discussions broke out about where they should settle. Some of the Pilgrims were all for "planting" near the mouth of the Pamet. While the site wasn't ideal, it did offer a safe place for small boats to harbor, land for farming, and excellent waters for fishing. Those in favor of settling at Cold Harbor also argued that they could not continue exploring in the winter without running the risk of losing men and equipment.

Bradford and some of the others argued against establishing their colony on the cape. Why should they settle for Cape Cod when a better location might be close by? Once settled, moving would be very difficult, if not impossible. Finally, they said, the water they had found on the cape was all in small ponds. How were they to know those ponds wouldn't go dry in summer?

As the Pilgrims tried to decide what their next move should be, Robert Coppin, one of the *Mayflower*'s mates who had been in New England, said he knew of a "great navigable river and good harbor" on the shore directly across Cape Cod Bay.[7] The Pilgrims decided to send a party of about ten men in the shallop to find the harbor that Coppin described. If they did not succeed, they would have no choice but to settle near Corn Hill.

These discussions took several days. During this period, one of the Pilgrim wives, Mrs. Susannah White, gave birth to a son, the first Englishman born in New England. She named the baby Peregrine, a flowery name that means Pilgrim in Latin. At about the same time, on December 5, fourteen-year-old Johnny Billington, the son of a family that was to cause Bradford a great deal of trouble in the years to come, almost put an end to all the Pilgrims' plans when he fired a musket belowdecks on the *Mayflower* within a few feet of a half-full keg of powder. As the gun roared, chunks of hot metal flew through the cabin and started a fire. Luckily or—as the Pilgrims would have said—thanks to Providence, some men were able to douse the flames before the powder keg exploded and sank the *Mayflower*.

The next day, December 6, Myles Standish led a party of sixteen men in search of the place described by Coppin. Weather conditions were miserable, windy and cold. "[T]he water froze on our clothes and made them many times like coats of iron," Bradford recounted. For safety, the explorers sailed along the coast of Cape Cod, instead of striking to the west, over open water. All day they sailed south. As night neared, they spied about a dozen Indians cutting up what Bradford called a "grampus"—perhaps a small whale—on the beach. Wanting to establish contact with the Natives, the explorers headed for the beach. By the time they reached shore, however, the Indians—members of the

Nauset tribe that inhabited most of Cape Cod–had run into the woods. Exhausted and freezing, Bradford and the others decided to make camp for the night.[8]

The next day, they, in Bradford's words, "went ranging up and down till the sun began to draw low" without establishing any contact with any of the Indians who must have been hiding in the woods watching their every move.[9] Again they spent the night on the beach, inside a barricade they erected for protection.

About midnight, the sleeping Englishmen were awakened by a "great and hideous cry" and by the frightened shouts of guards watching the beach. Standish and the others grabbed their muskets and quickly fired off a couple of shots, after which nothing more was heard. We can be sure that they spent the rest of the night in restless watching, waiting for the sun to rise. Not long before sunrise, the quiet was again broken by shouts that sounded to the Englishmen like "*Woach woach ha ha hach woach.*"[10] Nobody has ever been able to translate this cry as written by Bradford. In all likelihood, though, it was something like, "Kill the invaders!"

One of the Pilgrims who was outside the barricade immediately cried, "There are men! Indians! Indians!" and ran back inside the makeshift palisade, followed by a flight of arrows. The attack was short-lived. Standish and the others fired muskets at figures half-seen in the predawn light as arrows whizzed into the barricade. Even in the face of gunfire, one of the Indian warriors half-hid behind a tree within easy range of the Pilgrim muskets, loosing arrows at the people he viewed as interlopers on his land. Three muskets were fired in his direction, but still he stood his ground. Finally, one of the Pilgrims, probably Standish, shot and hit the tree near the Indian's head. "[A]fter which," Bradford said, "he gave an extraordinary shriek and away they went, all of them."[11]

The Indian attack at what is now known as First Encounter Beach seems to have convinced the Pilgrims that there was no hope of settling on Cape Cod. They set sail once again, determined to find the spot that Coppin claimed to have seen on an earlier visit.

In reality, while Coppin had visited New England, it seems he may never have visited Cape Cod Bay. It is thought, in fact, that what he described as a "good harbor" was Gloucester Harbor on Cape Ann. The Pilgrims, however, had no way of knowing that Coppin was mistaken and were willing to follow his lead. As they made their way up the coast, along the curving shore, their little boat was battered by one of the roaring gales known as a "nor'easter." "The seas were so great that we were much troubled and in great danger," Bradford said.[12]

Peering forward through wind-whipped spray, Coppin shouted that he saw the harbor ahead. At almost the same instant, a violent gust of wind struck the shallop's sail. With a sickening crack, the boat's mast fell into the water, dragging the heavy sail with it.

Frantic, the Pilgrims used their swords to hack at the lines that held the mast and sail tethered to the boat. Though they were lubbers, they knew the sail had become a drag that could easily turn them sideways to the raging waves. If that happened, the open boat would swamp and they would all be sent to the bottom or abandoned, freezing and without supplies, on the unfriendly shore. As they cut away the mast, other men leaped to the oars. Riding the flood tide, they raced toward what Coppin thought was a safe harbor. Suddenly, he spied white breakers crashing on the beach. For some reason, probably because he was terrified of the storm, he shouted for the oarsmen to steer for the shore, to ground the vessel, a move that would have been disastrous had not another of the *Mayflower*'s crewmen on the shallop seen the danger and screamed a warning.

Shivering, their clothes cloaked in ice, the Pilgrims heaved at their oars as the "lusty seaman" who had spied the danger ahead shouted for them to row or die.[13] Slowly, the shallop turned and clawed its way free of the breakers. Slowly, it made its way north until, in Bradford's words, "it pleased the Divine Providence that we fell upon a place of sandy ground, where our shallop did ride safe and secure. . . . "[14]

Almost by accident, and thanks only to the bravery of that unidentified "lusty seaman," the Pilgrims had made their way into Plymouth Harbor.

That night, the men in the shallop waded through freezing water to land on one of several small islands that dot the harbor. They managed to get a fire going and spent the night huddled miserably around its flames. In the morning, as they stood on the beach, the world looked new and fresh to them. The sun was shining, the sky blue. Since it was the Sabbath, they rested, dried their clothes, and, we may be sure, said many prayers of thanks.

The following day, December 11, they explored the harbor and found it deep and large enough to provide shelter to a fleet of ships. They also rowed to the mainland and went ashore. This first landing of the Pilgrims at what became Plymouth Colony is one of the most famous moments in American history. In legend—as reflected in most paintings and drawings of the event—

Pilgrim men, women, and children are shown stepping onto a large rock near the shore while benign Indians look on, smiling.

The reality was vastly different. There were no women or children present. If there were any Indians around, they were hidden in the woods. Those who came ashore may have stepped on what is famous today as Plymouth Rock, but nowhere in the histories written by the settlers is the rock ever mentioned. The men who struggled through the surf from their battered shallop to stand on the shores of Plymouth were themselves battered and bedraggled, their clothes torn and ragged. Most were sick, and all were hungry.

Once ashore, the Pilgrims continued exploring. "We marched also into the land," Bradford said, "and found diverse cornfields, and little running brooks, a place very good for situation."[15] Finally, the Pilgrims had found a place on which they could settle.

Pleased with what they had found—especially fields already cleared by Indians who were nowhere to be seen—the Pilgrim explorers were anxious to share their good news with their friends and loved ones. Quickly, they returned to the *Mayflower*.

As soon as William Bradford stepped on deck, he must have known something was wrong. It was, in all likelihood, Bradford's best and oldest friend who broke the news to him: While he was gone, Dorothy had somehow slipped overboard and drowned in the icy waters of Cape Cod Bay.

In his famous history of Plymouth, the only mention Bradford made of her death was in one of his notebooks on a page under the heading "Deaths," where he wrote, "Dorothy May wife to Mr. William Bradford."[16] It seems that he never wrote or spoke her name again.

Because of Bradford's silence, it is thought likely—though not certain—that Dorothy had committed suicide. Since suicide was, in those days, a terrible crime against God, that would explain why Bradford never mentioned her again. If she did kill herself, it was the desperate act of a lonely woman, far from her only child and the life she had known in Holland.

Whether Dorothy killed herself or died in an accident, Bradford must have felt terrible guilt and sadness. His mind must have been filled with doubts. If only he had allowed John to make the voyage as other young boys did . . . if only he had paid more attention to his wife . . . if only he had stayed on the *Mayflower* instead of going exploring . . . if only . . .

In any event, Bradford had little time to grieve. The Pilgrims had found a place to settle. Even as he mourned, those on the *Mayflower* were making ready for the short voyage from Cape Cod to the harbor that he and the others had found. There may have been a moment when he took a last look at the dark waters that had claimed her life, breathed a prayer for her soul, squared his shoulders, and turned to look across Cape Cod Bay to the place where he and the other Pilgrims would build their settlement.

THE TIME OF MOST DISTRESS

"But that which was most sad and lamentable was,
that in two or three months' time half
their company died. . . ."[1]

On December 16 the *Mayflower* headed across Cape
Cod Bay. By the time the Pilgrims left their anchorage
at the northern end of the cape, they may well have
decided to name their settlement Plymouth, perhaps
because Plymouth was the last harbor they had seen in
England or perhaps because they knew that was the
name given to the harbor and the land around it by
Captain John Smith when he visited the region in 1614.

In any event, they arrived too late in the day on
December 16 for any on board to go ashore. Since the
next day was the Lord's Day, they again put off their
landing. Finally, on December 18, an exploring party
made its way to shore.

The Pilgrims' first order of business was to deter-
mine exactly where to build their settlement. The spot
they chose was near a freshwater brook that emptied

into the harbor. This brook, now known as Town Brook, provided them with a supply of fresh water. Better yet, as they had discovered on their first visit, it was bordered by land that had been cleared by Indians and apparently abandoned, ready for planting. Of equal importance, the place chosen by Bradford and the others was at the bottom of a small hill where guard could be posted and cannon mounted for protection.

The Pilgrims must have been particularly pleased when they noticed that the brook formed a natural channel through the mudflats near shore, and that a large boulder stood just outside the mouth of that channel. This boulder provided the Pilgrims with something like a natural pier or landing stage. In all likelihood, one of the first things the Pilgrims did was build a walkway of squared logs running across the mudflats between the rock and the shore. With that walkway in place, the Pilgrims were able to hop from the shallop or the *Mayflower*'s longboat to the boulder and cross the wooden walkway to the beach without getting soaked.

This boulder is famous as Plymouth Rock. Although there is no evidence that there was ever a large-scale landing of the Pilgrims on Plymouth Rock, the rock still was important to the settlers of the colony. In fact, when the first town wharf was built in the mid-1700s, it was built directly over Plymouth Rock.

While the Pilgrims were in a hurry to get to work on their settlement—and the crew of the *Mayflower* wanted nothing but to dump their passengers on shore so they could return to England—bad weather delayed any work on Plymouth Town for several days. Finally, on December 23, twenty men came ashore with tools to start building homes. Soon the sound of axes and

*A very idealized portrayal of the Pilgrims
stepping onto Plymouth Rock.*

saws filled the air as the Pilgrims began constructing
rough shelters.

One of the most enduring myths about the Pilgrims
of Plymouth is that they lived in log cabins. The fact is
that there were no such cabins in America until about
1640 when settlers from Denmark arrived on the banks
of the Delaware River and used logs to build homes
like the dwellings in their homeland. The Pilgrims' very

first homes were one-room cottages built of twigs covered with mud–the same "wattle-and-daub" construction that was used for peasant cottages in England until the early seventeenth century. These tiny, rough shacks had fireplaces and chimneys made of clay-covered logs and roofs thatched with rushes that grew in the low lands near the shore.

Later, more permanent homes were made of squared timbers. To make these timbers, the Pilgrim men would dig a pit about 6 feet (2 meters) deep and lay a pine log across it. One man would stand in the pit, another outside on its edge. By pushing and pulling a two-handed saw they would rip the pine log into squared boards. These boards would then be placed side-by-side, vertically, to cover a frame made of stout oak beams. The inside walls of most homes were covered with clapboards, made by splitting cedar logs using an iron wedge known as a beetle, and a maul, or heavy hammer. These cedar clapboards were also popular in England and were exported by the Pilgrims as a way to pay off their debt to the Merchant Adventurers.

The Pilgrims quickly set to work building their homes, for they knew they must have shelter or they would perish in the New England cold. Even on Christmas Day–which the Saints did not celebrate because they believed that no one knew the exact date of Christ's birth–the Pilgrims, both Saints and Strangers, worked. "Monday, the 25th Day, we went on shore," Bradford said, "some to fell timber, some to saw, some to rive, and some to carry, so no man rested all that day."[2]

While some of the men worked building shelters, others cleared a road from the waterfront to the foot of the hill that overlooked the harbor. That road is now called Leyden Street. The hill, first known simply as the Mount, was later called Fort Hill and known still later as Burial Hill, since it became the site of Plymouth's burial ground.

Lots just 8 feet (2.4 meters) wide and about 50 feet (15 meters) deep were laid out on both sides of Leyden Street. Each person was allocated one lot, so that a family of four would have a parcel of land 32 feet (10 meters) wide and 50 feet deep. Single men were asked to attach themselves to a family, so the Pilgrims figured that they only needed nineteen houses to shelter everybody in the young colony. As things worked out, they needed far fewer.

Before construction started on any permanent dwellings, the Pilgrims set about building a common house, about 20 feet (6 meters) square, where supplies could be stored. By the end of the first week of January, this storehouse was almost completed, and families were busy building their own houses on both sides of Leyden Street.

As the Pilgrims struggled to gain a foothold in the New World, they suffered terribly. During the four months since their departure from England, they had had no fresh fruit or vegetables to eat. Now, on land, they had to get along on a diet largely of shellfish and game birds. While they had food, it was unappetizing to men and women used to hearty meals of beef, wheat bread, and beer. As a result, they were plagued by scurvy. Drenched by almost constant cold rains and weakened by the rigors of the ocean voyage, the change in their diet, and the scurvy, many came down with pneumonia. Others, it is thought, caught typhus, spread by lice on the *Mayflower*. Soon, almost everybody in the little settlement was sick.

In fact, during the early months of 1621, Plymouth was almost wiped out by disease. Of the one hundred and two passengers who arrived in Cape Cod, four died before the *Mayflower* anchored in Plymouth Harbor. In January and February, Bradford later said, "there died some times two or three of a day. . . . "[3] By the summer of 1621, fifty Pilgrims had died. Only a dozen of the original twenty-six heads of families survived; and just four of the original twelve unattached men or boys. Almost all the adult women perished. The younger boys and girls, perhaps because they were cared for by adults, fared better, and most survived. Conditions on the ship were no better than those on land. Indeed, many of the sick Pilgrims remained on board the ship, waiting for shelter to be completed ashore. In the ship's close quarters, the sickness that was killing Pilgrims on shore also ravaged the *Mayflower*'s officers and crew.

During these months, the storehouse was filled with the sick. Of the settlers, Bradford wrote, ". . . in the time of most distress, there was but six or seven sound persons" to care for the sick and dying.[4] Among those who nursed the ill, changed their filthy bedding, and fed them as best they could were William Brewster, Bradford's old mentor from Scrooby, and Myles Standish, the rough-and-tumble military man.

One of the chores the few healthy men had was to bury those who died. While there was no contact with the Indians who inhabited the region near what the Pilgrims called Plymouth Town, Bradford and the others felt certain that the local Native Americans were watching them carefully. To hide the fact that the little settlement was being scourged by disease, burials during these early months were done in secret, late at night, without any ceremony. Graves were unmarked, probably covered with brush, so the Indians could not tell how many of the settlers had died.

During this period, Bradford himself was laid low by illness. On January 11, while working in the fields, he was "vehemently taken with a grief and pain" so severe that it was feared he might die.[5] Moved to the common house, which by that time was crowded with the sick, he slowly started to recover.

Two nights later a spark from an open fire set the thatch roof of the makeshift hospital ablaze. Burning reeds and embers cascaded into the room where Bradford and other patients lay helpless, surrounded by open barrels of gunpowder and loaded muskets. Somehow, the few healthy men in the settlement managed to get the patients and the armament outside to safety. Though the building was saved, clothing and other valuable goods stored in the common house were lost.

Even as the Pilgrim colony was ravaged by illness, the handful of healthy men worked on permanent dwellings and struggled to prepare against the likelihood of an Indian attack. Slowly, the little community of Plymouth took shape. Houses were raised along Leyden Street, and the top of the hill overlooking the town was leveled.

In Bradford's history, nothing is said of the role that children played in these early days in Plymouth. However, in the seventeenth century, even three-year-old children were given easy chores–if for no other reason than to keep them busy and out of mischief. By the time boys and girls reached the age of six or seven, they were considered little adults. Boys undoubtedly were set to work gathering rushes to be used as thatch or shellfish from the shallows near the beach. Bigger boys, strong enough to handle a musket, probably hunted. Girls helped their mothers prepare meals, mend clothing, and do other household chores. There was no school in Plymouth for many years, but, knowing the Pilgrims, we can be sure there were home-taught lessons—at least in reading the Bible—when there was no work to do.

There were adventures, as well. Two of the young Pilgrim men, John Goodman and Peter Browne, set off in search of rushes, taking with them the settlement's spaniel and a mastiff. Suddenly, the dogs took off in pursuit of a deer. Goodman and Browne followed and soon were lost in the woods. After wandering for a day and night, they made it back to the settlement, but not before Goodman's feet were so swollen from the cold that his shoes had to be cut off. Just a few days later, he limped into the woods again with the spaniel. "A little way from the plantation," Bradford later wrote, "two great wolves ran after the dog. . . . " Unarmed, Goodman kept the wolves at bay with a stick while they, according to Bradford, "sat on their tails grinning at him. . . ."[6]

While the Pilgrims had been left alone by the Indians around Plymouth Town, Bradford and the other leaders knew it would be foolish not to be prepared in the event of trouble. In mid-February, Myles Standish was formally placed in charge of defense and authorized to command the other men. At the same time, the *Mayflower*'s captain, Christopher Jones, brought ashore several of the ship's large cannons and helped the Pilgrims install them on top of the Mount.

And so, with work and adventures and dying, the New England winter passed. Thankfully, spring came early in 1621. "Saturday, the 3rd of March," Bradford

wrote, "the wind was south, the morning misty, but towards noon warm and fair weather; the birds sang in
the woods most pleasantly."[7]

Friday, March 16, was another warm day. The Pilgrims decided to meet again to discuss military matters. They were gathered, probably in Leyden Street
where they could enjoy the mild weather and warm
breezes, when an Indian man suddenly entered the town
and walked unafraid down the street. He was, Bradford
said, "a tall, straight man, the hair of his head black, long
behind, only short before, none on his face at all. . . ." He
must have filled the Pilgrims, particularly the children,
with fear and wonder, for he was "stark naked, only a
leather about his waist . . . " and armed with a bow and
two arrows. Most amazing of all, though, was the way
he greeted the Pilgrims, for he walked boldly up to them
and said, in English, "Welcome."[8]

This Indian was Samoset. He was the sagamore—or
subchief—of a tribe that lived in Maine. For two decades
that part of America had been visited by English fishermen, and Samoset had met those seafarers and learned
to speak their language. He had also fallen in love with
English ways, for after greeting the Pilgrims he immediately asked for beer. Having none, the settlers gave
him instead "strong water (probably brandy) and bis-
cuit, and butter, and cheese, and pudding, and a piece
of mallard, all which he liked well. . . ."[9]

Samoset spent the afternoon answering the Pilgrims'
questions. He explained to them that he was a guest of
Massasoit, the sachem, or chief, of the Wampanoags,
the most powerful tribe in the region. He told them the
place they called Plymouth was called Patuxet by the
Indians. The lands on which they were building their

settlement had for many years been the home of a tribe of the same name, he said, adding that all those Indians except one had been wiped out by what he called the plague four years earlier.

Samoset spent that night in the home of one of the Pilgrims and departed the next morning, carrying a knife, a bracelet, and a ring as gifts. Two days later he was back again, this time with five Wampanoags who loved English food and drink as much as Samoset himself. On his next visit, on March 22, he was accompanied by an Indian brave named Squanto, the sole survivor of the plague that had devastated the place the Indians called Patuxet.

According to legend, Squanto was kidnapped by an English explorer in 1605 and taken to Plymouth, England, where he learned to speak and understand English. In 1614, having returned to New England as a translator for Captain John Smith, he was again kidnapped and taken, along with about twenty other Indian captives, to Spain, where he and the others were sold as slaves.

Perhaps because he spoke English, Squanto was purchased by a group of Spanish monks, who set him free, probably in 1616. From Spain he made his way to England and eventually to Newfoundland and then, in 1619 or early 1620, to Patuxet, his home. Expecting to find his family and friends and the village he had last seen six years earlier, he instead found only barren fields. All the Patuxet Indians in the village had died in an epidemic that swept much of coastal New England in 1617 and 1618.

We don't know what illness killed off the Indians. It may have been measles, smallpox, chicken pox, influenza, or some combination of diseases against which the Indians had no resistance. Whatever disease it was, it was brought ashore by European men and—in just three years—killed about 90 percent of the region's Indians. The lands that had once been home to thousands of Indians, a visitor wrote, were littered with "bones and skulls" of the victims.[10]

From his earliest days as a resident of the Pilgrim colony, Squanto was William Bradford's friend and companion, a man whom Bradford later called "a special instrument sent of God for their good beyond their expectation."[11] However, his arrival in the little settlement was quickly overshadowed when Massasoit, also called Ousamequin, or Yellow Feather, walked to the top of a rise on the far side of Town Brook and stood there with his brother, Quadequina, and about sixty braves. Massasoit was not only the chief of the Wampanoag but also the leader of all the native tribes in southeastern Massachusetts, including those living on Cape Cod.

Edward Winslow, dressed in armor and carrying a sword, crossed the brook with gifts for the chief. After delivering a speech of welcome, Winslow—a Saint who was to become one of Bradford's best friends and a trusted ambassador to the Native Americans who lived around Plymouth—volunteered to remain with Quadequina as a hostage while the sachem went to meet the other Pilgrim leaders.

According to a witness, Massasoit was "a very lusty [strong] man, in his best years, an able body, grave of countenance, and spare of speech." Like his warriors, he was almost naked, except for a fringed leather cloth round his waist. As a sign of his rank, he had a deerskin thrown over one shoulder and a large chain of bone beads around his neck. His face was painted "with a sad red like [mulberry]," while his companions were "in their faces, in part or in whole painted, some black, some red, some yellow, and some white, some with crosses, and other antic works; some had skins on them, and some naked; all [were] strong, tall men in appearance."[12]

Though the home where the Indian chief was led was not yet fully built, the settlers had hurriedly furnished it with a green rug and three or four cushions on which Massasoit could sit in comfort. Governor Carver, not wanting to appear subservient, let the sachem wait for a few moments before he entered to a trumpet salute and a drum roll. He was, no doubt, dressed in his finest robe of office, probably purple or blood-red.

Once Carver and Massasoit exchanged greetings, the Pilgrims offered the sachem what Bradford described as "friendly entertainment" including "strong water" (probably brandy).[13] Massasoit, we are told, drank "a great draught that made him sweat all the while after. . . ."[14]

With the "friendly entertainment" out of the way, Carver and Massasoit began to speak of peace, probably using Squanto as a translator. Quickly, the Indians and the settlers drew up a simple peace treaty, a mutual-assistance pact. According to its terms, the Pilgrims and Wampanoags promised not to "do hurt" to one another. If the peace was broken by an Indian, he was to be sent to the settlement for punishment, and viceversa. Indians coming to visit Plymouth were to leave their weapons outside the settlement; and the Pilgrims were to enter Sowams, Massasoit's village, unarmed. In addition, each party to the treaty promised to help the other in the case of an attack by any outsider.

In need of allies, both the Wampanoags and the Pilgrims were happy about the treaty. Indeed, the pact

*The famous meeting of Governor John Carver and
Massasoit, sachem of the Wampanoags.*

agreed to in early 1621 remained unbroken for more
than 50 years, until after Massasoit's death.

This first meeting between the leaders of the colony
and Massasoit was a success. Indeed, if anything, the
Indians seemed to be overly fond of the Pilgrims or at
least of Pilgrim food. Large numbers of Native Americans would come to the tiny settlement where the Pilgrims would give them food they could not afford to

part with. Eventually, this became a problem that the leaders would have to deal with.

Not long after the signing of the treaty, the first court trial in Plymouth was held. At that trial, John Billington, the father of the young boy who had almost blown up the *Mayflower*, was tried on charges that he refused to obey a lawful order given to him by Captain Myles Standish. After being sentenced to "have his neck and heels tied together," Billington pleaded for mercy and, Bradford said, "it being his first offence, he [was] forgiven."[15]

The mood in the little colony must have been optimistic. Though food was scarce, the great illness had come to an end. The planting time was near and it was just a matter of time before their crops would be ready for harvest. There was peace between the Pilgrims and the Wampanoags. In fact, things were so good that on April 5, after five months in the New World, Captain Jones of the *Mayflower* ordered her anchor broken free and her sails unfurled for the return voyage to England.

Jones and the men on the *Mayflower* must have breathed prayers of thanks as the ship made her way out of Plymouth Harbor. During the winter months, about half the men on board the vessel had breathed their last. Now, finally, the survivors were homeward bound.

Remarkably, as the *Mayflower* prepared to sail away from Plymouth, none of the Pilgrims—neither Saints nor Strangers—asked to be taken on board, though they had reason to abandon the colony. That these survivors chose to remain in Plymouth is a testament to their courage and faith. Many English settlers, both at Roanoke and Jamestown, had fled for England as soon as they had an opportunity. But the Pilgrims remained, even though they had experienced the deaths of family members and loved ones, and even though they knew it would be long years–if ever–before they enjoyed anything like comfort or knew anything but back-breaking, sunrise-to-sunset work.

If the Pilgrims needed any reminder of how precarious life was in Plymouth, they got it quickly. Just a week or so after the *Mayflower* sailed away, Governor Carver was working when, Bradford said, he suddenly "came out of the field very sick, it being a hot day. He complained greatly of his head and lay down, and within a few hours his senses failed, so as he never spake more till died . . . a few days after." The death of the respected leader, he added, "was much lamented and caused great heaviness among them. . . ."

Carver was buried in what Bradford called "the best manner they could, with some volleys of shot by all that bore arms." There was no religious ceremony, since that would have smacked of the same pomp the Pilgrims associated with the Anglican and Catholic churches. Nor was there a ceremony just a few weeks later when Carver's wife died, probably of a broken heart.[16]

Immediately after Governor Carver's simple burial, William Bradford, then thirty-one years of age, was elected governor of Plymouth Colony. Still weak from the illness he had suffered soon after landing in Plymouth, he asked for and was given an assistant, Isaac Allerton. The governorship of Plymouth was a position that Bradford was to hold for most of the remainder of his life.

Bradford wrote only a few words about his election in his history of the colony, and in the third person, as if he was reluctant to talk about himself.

"William Bradford was chosen governor in [Carver's] stead," he wrote, ". . . which I note here once [and] for all."[17]

With his election as governor of Plymouth Colony, William Bradford, the largely self-educated yeoman's son from England, a man who might have spent his life tending sheep, stepped into the void left by the death of John Carver and earned his place in history.

THE FIRST THANKSGIVING

"Our harvest being gotten in, our governor sent
four men on fowling, that so we might after a more
special manner rejoice together after we have
gathered the fruit of our labors."[1]

It was spring when William Bradford took office as the
governor of Plymouth. It was a time for a new beginning. Warm, gentle winds blew across the land. Trees
were green, and the air was filled with the scent of growing things and the sounds of singing birds.

There was a new beginning, too, in the affairs of the
colony. With Bradford's election as governor, the leadership of the colony was in the hands of younger men.
Bradford was thirty-one, while his assistant, Allerton,
was about thirty-four. Myles Standish was thirty-six, and
Edward Winslow, an able diplomat in dealings with the
Indians, was younger still, just twenty-six. Of the older
men who had been the leaders until that time, only
Bradford's good friend William Brewster was still alive
and in Plymouth. Carver was dead. Robert Cushman,
the man who had worked so hard to obtain financing

for the venture, was in England, and Pastor John Robinson, the spiritual leader of the Saints, was in Holland.

It is important to note that none of the young men who led Plymouth were officers of the church. It is likely that Bradford and the other Saints remembered all too well what could happen when the church and state were ruled by one person, as in England. Without ever formally stating the idea that church and state should be kept separate, they seem to have made the separation of church and state—so important to the American system of democracy—central to their colony's government.

It should also be noted that these young leaders were widowers. Dorothy Bradford had died while the *Mayflower* was anchored in Cape Cod Bay. Standish's wife and Allerton's and Winslow's wives had died during the terrible winter months. Given positions of leadership, these younger men, probably as a way of dealing with their losses and sadness, turned their full energies toward the service of Plymouth.

Suddenly, Bradford said later, the colony was infused with new energy. It was as if, he explained, the warm spring weather "put . . . new life into them."[2] Squanto quickly proved himself to be an invaluable friend. He showed them how to catch "fat and sweet" eels.[3] He taught the English farmers that the best time to plant corn was in the spring when the new leaves of white oak trees were just opening and each leaf was "as big as the ear of a mouse."[4] He showed them how to plant corn and how to catch hundreds, thousands of alewifes, little herringlike fish, they could use as fertilizer to make the corn grow tall and fat.

In early May, Edward Winslow and Susanna White, whose husband had died during the winter, were married. This marriage, and the sight of the corn beginning to send up green shoots, must have done wonders for the Pilgrims' spirits as they recuperated from the terrible winter.

During this time, Wampanoag braves, often with their entire families in tow, regularly visited the settlement, where they would eat biscuits and butter and drink the settlers' dwindling supply of beer and spirits. It was soon obvious to Bradford that the drain on the colony's supplies had to be stopped. On June 10, he dispatched Winslow and Stephen Hopkins, one of the Strangers, to visit Massasoit. With Squanto as a guide, the Pilgrims made their way to the Indian village of Sowams (now Warren, Rhode Island), about 25 miles (40 kilometers) south of Plymouth.

At Sowams, Winslow and Hopkins found terrible evidence of the devastating plague that had killed so many of the coastal Indians of Massachusetts about three years before. They reported what they found to Bradford, who included it in his history. "They found . . . the people not many, being dead and abundantly wasted in the late, great mortality," he wrote. "They not being able to bury one another, their skulls and bones were found in many places lying still above the ground where their houses and dwellings had been, a very sad spectacle to behold."[5]

Meanwhile, the message carried by Winslow was simple. While the Pilgrims wanted to remain friends with the Wampanoags, they could no longer tolerate the Indians' "disorderly coming" to Plymouth. Of course, he added, any who had beaver skins were welcome to come "truck," or trade, at any time, in any number.[6]

To soften his message, Winslow presented Massasoit with a "horseman's coat of red cotton, . . . laced with white lace" and a copper chain he could use to identify any special emissaries he sent to the settlement.[7] After making a promise to the Pilgrim ambassadors that his men would "no more pester you as they have done," Massasoit made a long speech, ending his oration with a vow that he was "King James his man."[8]

During the trek to Sowams and the lengthy meeting with Massasoit, the Pilgrims had gone hungry. With their business out of the way, they expected the Indians to provide them with a meal. Unfortunately, they had chosen a bad time to visit Sowams, for there was no food in the village. Apparently embarrassed by his inability to entertain his visitors, Massasoit insisted that Winslow and Hopkins share his royal bed with him and his wife that night. "He laid us on the bed with himself and his wife," Winslow later wrote, "they at the one end and we at the other, it being only planks laid a foot from the ground, and a thin mat upon them." If that wasn't bad enough, two of Massasoit's men soon climbed into the already crowded bed and began singing themselves to sleep. During the long night, Winslow and Hopkins were bitten by fleas and lice. When the dawn came, Winslow said, they were "worse weary of our lodgings than of our journey."[9]

Finally, in the early afternoon of their second day at Sowams, the Pilgrims were served a meal, but since it consisted only of two boiled bass for about forty people, they were left almost starving. Making an excuse, they left for Plymouth early the next morning, afraid, Winslow said, "that if we should stay any longer, we should not be able to recover home for want of strength."[10]

About the time of this visit to Sowams, another Indian became an ally of the Pilgrims when Hobomok, one of Massasoit's warriors, came to live in Plymouth. Not surprisingly, Squanto and Hobomok soon became rivals. Bradford, proving that he could be a wily politician, encouraged this rivalry by showing favor to Squanto, while Hobomok became an ally of Myles Standish. In this way, Bradford said, he hoped to obtain "better intelligence [from them] and make them both more diligent."[11]

Also about this time, young Johnny Billington–the boy who almost blew up the *Mayflower* when the ship was anchored in Cape Cod Bay–got lost in the woods near the settlement. After five days of wandering, he made his way to an Indian village at Manomet, on Cape Cod. From there, the Indians sent him on to the Nausets, the same tribe that had attacked the Pilgrims at First Encounter Beach. The Nausets, in turn, notified Massasoit that they were playing hosts to one of the Pilgrim children.

When Bradford learned that young Johnny was in the Indians' hands, he probably thought about leaving him there. The family was, he said, "one of the profanest families amongst them" and a constant source of trouble.[12] Still, he knew he couldn't leave young John with the Nausets, and so, with Squanto as his interpreter, Bradford led a small group of men in the shallop to the Indian village near the site of present-day Eastham on Cape Cod. There he met with Aspinet, the sachem of the Nausets, who turned Johnny over to the Pilgrims. At the same time, Bradford made arrangements to pay for the corn the Pilgrims had dug up when they first explored the region in late 1620. In that way, he not only discharged the Pilgrims' debt to the Indians but also made Aspinet an ally.

During these months, not all of Bradford's attention was focused on the Indians. He oversaw the day-to-day running of Plymouth as crops were tended and seven plank houses were built, probably by John Alden, the Stranger hired as a carpenter and barrel maker.

As fall approached, with the settlement beginning to thrive, Bradford turned his thoughts to establishing profitable trade with the local Native Americans. In mid-September 1622, he sent Standish and a party of about a dozen men, including Squanto, to the Massachusetts Bay region, where the Pilgrims made contact with the Massachusetts Indians and began to trade for beaver that could be used to pay the Pilgrims' debts to the Merchant Adventurers.

By the time this trading expedition returned to Plymouth, the harvest was ready for gathering. Bradford and the other Pilgrims knew they faced another difficult winter, but they also knew they had much for which they could be thankful. They were, Bradford wrote, "all well recovered in health and strength and had all things in good plenty." They didn't have all the beef and beer they desired, but they did have corn and a "good store" of cod and bass and other fish. As the days grew shorter and winter neared, game was plentiful and the Pilgrims were able to shoot ducks, wild turkey, and venison.[13]

Bradford, probably remembering the Dutch custom of having an annual day of thanksgiving on October 3, the anniversary of Leyden's deliverance from a siege mounted by the Spanish, ordered the Pilgrims to set aside a day to give thanks for all the blessings the colony had received in the wilderness. The date of this first Thanksgiving Day in America is uncertain, but it was probably sometime in mid-October.

Bradford did not describe this first Thanksgiving in his history. Fortunately, Winslow did, in a letter to a friend. This letter was included in a history of the colony's first year, coauthored by Bradford and Winslow and published in London in 1622. Today that history is known as "Mourt's Relation" because it included a preface signed by "G. Mourt," probably a pen name for George Morton, a friend of the Pilgrims who had arranged to have the brief report printed as a pamphlet.

A painting of the first Thanksgiving. The helmeted man on the right is surely Myles Standish, and the elderly man with the puritan collar on the left might be William Brewster.

"Our harvest being gotten in," Winslow wrote in his letter, "our governor sent four men on fowling, that so we might after a more special manner rejoice together after we had gathered the fruit of our labors. They four in one day killed as much fowl as, with a little help beside, served the company almost a week."[14] As the fowl were being roasted, about ninety Indians made their way to the settlement. Massasoit, no doubt dressed in his fine red coat, was there with his favorite wife. As their contribution to the feast, the Wampanoags supplied five freshly killed deer. There were no cranberries, but lots of raspberries, gooseberries, strawberries, and plums.

For three days, the Pilgrims and Indians celebrated together under the trees on the banks of Plymouth Harbor. The Pilgrims displayed their marksmanship with their muskets, while the Indians showed off their skill with bows and arrows. Though we don't know for sure, it is likely that Indian and Pilgrim children played together and probably tussled while the adults ran foot races and held wrestling matches and sat under the maples and oaks with their bright-colored leaves, groaning a bit from eating and drinking too much.

This first Thanksgiving celebrated in America must have been a joyful time for William Bradford as he surveyed what was his domain. Fortunately, he had no way of knowing that the joy he felt would be short-lived and that the abundance the Pilgrims celebrated would soon be nothing more than a memory.

TROUBLES FROM WITHIN AND WITHOUT

"... I fear you must stand on your legs and trust (as they say) to God and yourselves."[1]

In mid-November, just a few weeks after the first Thanksgiving feast, an Indian brave ran into Plymouth Town with the news that a ship had been spotted off Cape Cod, apparently making her way to the Pilgrim settlement.

There was a chance that the ship was a supply vessel sent by the Adventurers. For all the Pilgrims knew, however, it could just as easily be a French privateer sent to pillage the colony and to drive the settlers off the land or a Dutch ship of war sent to protect that nation's claims in the New World. Knowing it was better to be prepared for danger, Bradford quickly ordered men to stand watch on top of the Mount and the cannon and muskets made ready for battle.

Soon, the strange vessel—the first to visit the colony since the *Mayflower*'s departure—was spied making her way past the headland known as the Gurnet and into

Plymouth Bay. As the ship hove into view, Bradford ordered one of the big guns guarding the settlement fired as a signal to those working in the fields. In moments, Edward Winslow later said, "every man, yea boy, that could handle a gun, were ready, with full resolution that, if she were an enemy, we would stand in our just defence, not fearing them."[2]

Finally, as the ship neared shore, one of the watchers was able to make out a white and red ensign–St. George's Cross–waving from the masthead. The ship was English. She was the *Fortune* sent by the London Adventurers with thirty-four recruits for the colony.

At first, Bradford was filled with joy when he saw the men and women sent over by the Adventurers. Some on board had been among those who were forced to turn back when the *Speedwell* proved unseaworthy. Others were relatives of those already in Plymouth. Edward Winslow's brother John was among the passengers, as was Jonathan Brewster, William Brewster's son. Robert Cushman, who had been so helpful before the Pilgrims left Holland, was also a passenger. Also on board were Thomas Prence, who was to serve several terms as the colony's governor; and a man named Philip de la Noye, an ancestor of President Franklin Delano Roosevelt.

Bradford's joy at seeing the newcomers, however, turned to worry as soon as he discovered that they had brought no supplies with them from England. "[T]here was not so much as biscuit-cake or any other victuals for them, neither had they any bedding . . . ; nor pot nor pan to dress any meat in; nor overmany clothes . . . ," he said. Though he was glad of the "addition of strength" to the colony, he said, he wished "all of them better furnished with provisions."[3]

There was good reason for Bradford's concern. The arrival of the newcomers meant that Plymouth once again faced starvation. Food supplies that could have fed fifty persons from November until the next planting season had to be stretched to feed almost twice that number. Immediately, Bradford decreed that the settlers would have to go on half-rations, hoping the food supplies would last until provisions arrived from England.

A shortage of food wasn't the only problem Bradford had to deal with after the *Fortune*'s passengers joined the colony. Housing, too, was scarce. There was no answer but to jam the newcomers into the already crowded houses that lined Leyden Street. Eighty-four men, women, and children had to live in the eleven one-room houses the Pilgrims had built since landing in December 1620. Lean-tos were added to the rears and sides of some of the cottages.

Meanwhile, though the *Fortune* carried no supplies to speak of, she did deliver a formal patent giving the colony legal status. This patent had been requested in a letter sent back to England on the *Mayflower*. Signed by the men who made up the Council for New England, a newly formed governing body responsible for the settlement of the region that now roughly comprises Massachusetts, Maine, New Hampshire, and Connecticut, the patent confirmed the Mayflower Compact and promised that after seven years each settler would be awarded 100 acres (40 hectares) of land.

The ship also brought a nasty letter from Thomas Weston—the colony's chief financial backer—to the Pilgrims. Weston chastised the settlers for not sending back any cargo to England on board the *Mayflower*. The letter also warned the Pilgrims that all help would be cut off if they did not load the *Fortune* with profitable goods, make an account of how they had spent money already advanced to them by the Adventurers, and send back a signed copy of the contract they had refused to sign before leaving England.

Seething with anger, Bradford quickly wrote a reply in which he recounted all the troubles the Pilgrims had encountered in the short time at Plymouth. To be sure, he said, Weston and the other Adventurers might lose money. But Carver and many other "honest and industrious" men had lost their lives. Lives, Bradford said, that "cannot be valued at any price."[4]

When the *Fortune* departed after about a month in Plymouth Harbor, in the ship's hold was a valuable cargo of otter and beaver skins along with cedar boards used for decorative purposes in England. That cargo would have paid about half of what the Pilgrims owed to Weston and the other Adventurers. Unfortunately for the Pilgrims, the cargo never made it to England. A French privateer captured the *Fortune* off the French coast and stole her cargo.

Somehow, when the crew of the privateer searched the ship, they overlooked papers that Cushman had been given before he left Plymouth. Among those papers was the manuscript of "Mourt's Relation," which was meant to attract new settlers to Plymouth. For that reason, it did not include any description of the sickness that almost wiped out the colony in the winter of 1620–1621. It did, however, provide England with its first account of the settlement. It is still considered one of the best sources for information about the everyday lives of the Pilgrims and of the Indians who lived near Plymouth.

Soon after the *Fortune*'s departure, the winter wind began to howl, the temperature plummeted, and snow blanketed the ground. For days or weeks at a time, the Pilgrims must have spent almost all their free hours inside their small, dark homes, huddled near the open hearths, shivering from the cold.

Still, as 1621 ended and 1622 began, Bradford faced one crisis after another.

The first crisis arose when a Narragansett Indian brave—a member of one of the tribes with whom the Pilgrims had not made peace—walked boldly into Plymouth carrying a bundle of arrows tied together by a snakeskin. This strange package, Squanto and Hobomok told Bradford, was a challenge from the Narragansetts: a signal that they wanted war.

Bradford responded quickly. He sent a message to the Narragansetts that if they wanted war, "they might begin when they would." The Pilgrims, he added, "had done them [the Narragansetts] no wrong, neither did they fear them or should they find them unprovided."[5] He then placed a handful of musket balls and some gunpowder inside the snakeskin and sent the package—a symbolic warning of his own—back to Canonicus, the Narragansett sachem.

Bradford's quick response must have convinced Canonicus that Plymouth was too strong to attack, for his threat was not repeated. The Narragansett warning, however, made Bradford wary. Not wanting to be caught unprotected, he ordered the building of a stout, wooden palisade around the settlement. The palisade around Plymouth was about 11 feet (3 meters) high, made of logs placed side by side. It enclosed the town's houses and their individual garden plots as well as a large portion of the Mount.

No sooner was this major project finished than serious trouble arose within the settlement. Squanto, who
had been a great help to the colony, started a rumor
that Massasoit and his warriors were going to attack
Plymouth. He apparently thought that if he could make
trouble between the Pilgrims and Wampanoags he
would be even more important to the settlers than
Massasoit.

As soon as Massasoit learned of Squanto's treachery, the chief came to Plymouth and demanded that
Bradford turn Squanto over to him in accordance with
the peace treaty. Bradford knew that if he delivered
Squanto to the enraged Wampanoag chief he would
surely be executed. Unable to bring himself to give up
Squanto for punishment, he tried to placate Massasoit
by explaining that Squanto had already been severely
punished for his crime.

Massasoit seemed to accept what Bradford said but
soon grew angry again and sent a messenger to Plymouth renewing his demand that the Pilgrims live up to
the terms of the peace treaty. This messenger, Edward
Winslow said, was accompanied by several braves carrying beaver pelts, which they offered to Bradford if he
would turn over Squanto to them so they could cut off
his head and hands and carry those grisly proofs of his
execution to Massasoit.

As much as Bradford wanted to protect Squanto,
he knew he had to agree to Massasoit's demands under
the terms of the peace agreement. Not to do so would
be foolish, for if Massasoit decided to wage war against
the tiny settlement, the Wampanoags would wipe Plymouth out. Reluctantly, he called for Squanto and prepared to hand him over to his executioners. Winslow,
who witnessed the whole affair, described what hap-

pened next: "But at the instant when [Bradford] was ready to deliver [Squanto] into the hands of his executioners," he wrote, "a boat was seen at sea . . . before our town. . . ."[6]

As he had done when the *Fortune* was spotted nearing the colony, he ordered the Pilgrims to prepare for an attack. At the same time, he told Massasoit's messengers that they would have to leave without Squanto. "Mad with rage," Winslow said, "and impatient at delay, they [the Indians] departed in 'great heat.'"[7]

The arrival of the strange boat in Plymouth Harbor saved Squanto's life, for Massasoit eventually got over his anger, perhaps satisfied when his messengers told him that Bradford was, indeed, ready to surrender his Indian friend for execution.

The vessel that saved Squanto's life, meanwhile, proved to be a ship's boat from the *Sparrow*, a fishing vessel belonging to none other than Thomas Weston. On the boat were seven passengers sent by him to plant a settlement outside the control of the Pilgrim leaders. In a letter to the Pilgrims, Weston, in the high-handed fashion that was his trademark, asked them to provide the newcomers with food and shelter and to give them seed corn. The letter also contained the news that two more ships were on their way to Plymouth with even more colonists for Weston's new settlement.

In late June 1622, these ships—the *Charity* and the *Swan*—arrived. On board were sixty men sent by Weston. Just as had been the case with the newcomers who arrived on the *Fortune*, these new settlers—described by Bradford as "an unruly company"—brought no food or other supplies.[8] Bradford had no choice but to see to it that they were fed, sheltered, and cared for until they were ready to establish their own settlement.

Almost on the heels of the *Charity* and the *Swan*, yet another vessel made her way into Plymouth Harbor, delivering a message from Captain John Huddleston, the master of an English fishing vessel bound from Virginia to the cod banks near Maine. In his letter, addressed to his "friends, countrymen and neighbors,"[9] Huddleston told of the terrible massacre of almost four hundred men, women, and children by Indians in Virginia just a few months earlier. He warned the Pilgrims to be on guard.

Bradford immediately took Huddleston's advice to heart. He ordered the building of a fort on the Mount, overlooking the settlement and the approach to the harbor. Completed about a year later, the fort was constructed of stout, squared oak timbers. It was a one-story building with a flat roof on which the cannons taken from the *Mayflower* were mounted. For decades this building served as a town hall, jail, courthouse, and meetinghouse for the Pilgrim church services.

Isaak de Rasieres, a visitor to Plymouth a few years after the fort was built, described the scene on a typical Sabbath when the Pilgrim Fathers and their families gathered for services in the fort.

> *They assemble by beat of drum, each with his musket or firelock . . . ; they have their cloaks on, and place themselves in order, three abreast, and are led by a sergeant. . . .*
>
> *Behind comes the Governor, in a long robe; beside him on the right hand, comes the preacher [William Brewster, ruling elder of the church] with his cloak on, and on the left hand, the captain [Standish] with his side-arms and cloak on . . . , and so they march in good order, and each sets his*

arms down near him. Thus they are constantly on
their guard night and day."[10]

Indeed, this Pilgrim habit of going to church armed
would continue at Plymouth for about fifty years after
those early services.

Huddleston's friendly letter, meanwhile, led
Bradford to believe that the ship's captain might be willing to supply the colony–now desperately in need of
food–with provisions. He quickly dispatched Edward
Winslow in the shallop to see whether he could obtain
food. At the fishing grounds off the coast of Maine,
Winslow found a large fleet of English ships, including
Huddleston's. The captains of this fishing fleet were
much more ready to supply the colony than were the
Merchant Adventurers in London. Soon Winslow sailed
back to Plymouth with what Bradford called "some good
quantity" of supplies. Still, he noted, since the supplies
had to be divided among more than one hundred men,
women, and children, it "came to . . . but a quarter of a
pound of bread a day to each person." It was, though,
enough to keep them alive, barely, until the harvest.[11]

As the summer of 1622 was nearing its end, Bradford
and the other Pilgrims must have been counting the
days until they could reap their harvest. Perhaps they
were even looking forward to another time of plenty
and another Thanksgiving celebration. Instead, they
were disappointed, for this harvest of 1622 was much
smaller than they had expected. In fact, although
Bradford wrote that "all had their hungry bellies filled,"
it seems that the harvested grain was eaten almost immediately. The crop would have been greater, Bradford
explained, had the Pilgrims not been so weak from
hunger that they were unable to properly tend their

crops. Weston's men, still in Plymouth at that time and still being cared for by the Pilgrims, made matters worse by stealing corn even "before it became scarce eatable."[12]

In fact, the situation in Plymouth was critical. There was a lack of corn for eating and, worse, seed for planting. ". . . [I]t well appeared that famine must still ensue . . . ," Bradford said. By that time, he must have wondered if the Pilgrims would ever be free of the threat of starvation, for a lack of seed corn meant that hunger would continue for the foreseeable future. He must have spent much time in prayer, asking God to provide for the Pilgrims. Suddenly, in August, it appeared that God heard his prayers, for unexpected help appeared. "Behold now another providence of God," he wrote, "a ship comes into the harbor."[13]

This ship was the *Discovery*, an English vessel sent to trade with Indians between Massachusetts and Virginia and now on her way back to London. In her hold, Bradford soon learned, was a good supply of beads and knives and other trinkets, which he knew could be traded to the Indians for food. Though the ship's captain was willing to sell the Pilgrims merchandise, he charged almost ten times as much for the goods as they were worth. Bradford, however, had no choice.

While the *Discovery* was anchored in Plymouth Bay, one of her passengers, John Pory, the secretary of the Virginia Colony, came ashore. After meeting some of the colonists and looking around the little settlement, he was so impressed that he later wrote several letters filled with kind words about Plymouth Town and the Pilgrims themselves. "[C]oncerning the quality of the people," he wrote, "how happy were it for our people in [Virginia], if they were as free from wickedness and vice as these are in this place."[14]

❧ 11 ❧

INDIAN TROUBLES

"It is . . . a thing more glorious, in men's eyes,
than pleasing in God's . . . , to be a terrour to
poor barbarous people."[1]

While the master of the *Discovery* had, in Edward
Winslow's phrase, made the Pilgrims "pay largely" for
goods to trade with, the situation in the colony would
have been "worse than ever it had been, or after was . . . ,
not having any means left to . . . trade."[2]

Hoping to obtain a good supply of food, Bradford
agreed to a plan put forward by Weston's men, who by
that time had established their own settlement in
Wessagusset. That plan called for the Pilgrims to supply the trade goods, while the Wessagusset group supplied a large coastal vessel that could make its way
around Cape Cod, calling on Indian villages. In late
September this expedition, including Bradford and
Squanto, set out.

Eventually, the settlers were able to trade for a total
of twenty-eight casks, called hogsheads, of corn and

beans—enough food to stave off starvation, at least for a time. However, the journey was a tragic one, at least as far as Bradford was concerned, for in the midst of the expedition, Squanto suddenly became ill. According to Bradford, his friend "fell sick of an Indian fever, bleeding much at the nose. . . ." Within a day or two, the man who served as the "tongue" for the English of Plymouth, the last survivor of the Patuxet tribe, was dead.

Before he died, Squanto asked Bradford to pray for him so that "he might go the Englishmen's God in Heaven." He also bequeathed his few belongings to his English friends so that they might remember him. His death, Bradford wrote, was "a great loss" to the entire colony.[3] In all likelihood, Bradford felt a mixture of sorrow at the death of his friend, without whom the Pilgrims would have perished in the wilderness, and joy that Squanto had converted to Christianity before his death.

As food supplies ran low again and the winter weather turned cruel, the situation in the settlement became desperate. For some reason—perhaps the supplies of powder and shot were low or game was scarce—the Pilgrims had no success hunting. They were forced to survive on edible roots they called "ground nuts," clams, and any other food they could forage.

As bad as things were in Plymouth, though, they were much worse in Wessagusset. The settlers there quickly ate all the supplies they had obtained on the trading voyage. With those gone, they sold their clothes and blankets, worked as servants to the Indians in exchange for food, or stole what they wanted. Soon many were dying of starvation. "One," Bradford reported, "in gathering shellfish was so weak as he stuck fast in the mud and was found dead in the place."[4]

Starving and desperate, the Wessagusset men decided to attack their Indian neighbors and to take the food they needed by force. Before mounting an attack, however, John Sanders, the leader of Weston's settlement, sent a letter to Bradford asking him what he thought of their plans. Bradford, knowing an attack against the Indians near Wessagusset would undoubtedly invite retaliation and cause the deaths of all the Englishmen in the region, convinced Sanders not to resort to violence. Instead of stealing from the Indians, he said in a letter to Sanders, the Wessagusset men should learn–like the Pilgrims–to live on "ground nuts, clams, muscles [mussels], and such other things as naturally the country afforded, and which did and would maintain strength. . . ." It would be better, he added, to "continue their peace [with the Indians]; upon which course they might with good conscience desire and expect a blessing of God."[5]

Meanwhile, the plan to attack the Indians was not a well-kept secret. In fact, some of the Wessagusset men told the Indians about the plan, hoping, no doubt, to obtain food in exchange for the information. As news of the planned raid spread through the tribes to the north of Plymouth, the Indians determined to attack the settlers first, at Wessagusset and then at Plymouth.

It was only by good fortune that the Pilgrims discovered what the Indians to the north were planning. In March 1623, Bradford learned that Massassoit was gravely sick and wanted to see Winslow, who by that time was both liked and trusted by the sachem and the Wampanoag people. In Massassoit's village on the shores of Narragansett Bay, wrote Winslow, he found Massassoit in a crowded house, surrounded by women who "chafed his arms, legs, and thighs" to help his circulation while other members of his tribe, probably medicine men, were in the "midst of their charms for him, making . . . a hellish noise."[6]

Winslow soon decided that Massassoit's problem was nothing more than a bout of constipation, though it must have been a serious case indeed, since the sachem was unable to see when Winslow arrived. For two days, he treated the chief with medicines he had carried from Plymouth and doses of duck broth and cornmeal boiled with strawberry leaves and sassafras root. Finally, Winslow reported, the chief recovered his strength and was "able to sit upright of himself."

Cured, Massasoit thanked Winslow again and again. "Now I see the English are my friends and love me," he said, "and whilst I live I will never forget this kindness they have showed me."[7] Massassoit's friendship prompted the sachem to pass on news of the planned attack against the Englishmen, and he also advised the Pilgrims to "kill the [Massachusetts], who were the authors of this intended mischief."[8]

On his return to Plymouth, Winslow reported what he had learned to Bradford. Within just a few days, as if to add weight to what Massassoit had said, one of the Wessagusset settlers came to the colony with the news that the English settlers "would be all knocked in the head shortly."[9]

On March 23, 1623, at the regular annual court day—the forerunner of the modern New England town meeting—Bradford told the other Pilgrims all he knew of the Indian plot. Though it is likely that he already had decided to strike the Massachusetts Indians before they mounted an attack against Wessagusset, he was unwilling to put that decision into action "without the consent of the body of the company."[10]

If Bradford wanted the Pilgrims as a group to decide the Indians' fate, he was disappointed. All in Plymouth knew, or at least believed, that if they allowed the Indians to attack and kill the men of Wessagusset then all the English in the region would be killed. The Pilgrims, however, were unwilling collectively to take responsibility for mounting an attack against the Massachusetts Indians. After a lengthy debate they asked Bradford to make the decision himself after consulting with Allerton and Captain Standish.

Bradford quickly decided that Standish, with eight men, would assassinate the ringleaders of the plot to attack the English—braves identified by Standish as Wituwamat and Pecksuot. Bradford also ordered Standish to bring Wituwamat's head back to Plymouth so the Indian's head could serve as a "warning and terror" to any other Indians who might consider attacking the English.[11]

Standish and his men soon made their way to Weston's colony. There the small Pilgrim army spent several days watching and waiting for an opportunity to strike. During this time, Winslow reported, both Wituwamat and Pecksuot insulted and threatened Standish, as if they wanted to start a fight. Wituwamat went so far as to sharpen his knives "before [Standish's] face" and brag that his knife blades would soon "eat" English blood.[12]

On their third day at Wessagusset, Standish managed to get Pecksuot, Wituwamat, the eighteen-year-old brother of Wituwamat, and another brave alone in the house where the Pilgrim soldiers were lodged. Once the Indians were inside, he gave a signal to his men. Immediately, the Pilgrims attacked. Pecksuot was the first to fall. According to Winslow, Standish snatched the Indian's knife from around his neck and "with much struggling, killed him therewith. . . ."[13] While Standish struggled with Pecksuot, the soldiers with him stabbed Wituwamat and the other brave while Wituwamat's brother was captured and hanged.

Winslow described this onesided battle in chilling language. "[I]t is incredible how many wounds these two pineses [the subchiefs Wituwamat and Pecksuot] received before they died, not making any fearful noise, but catching at their weapons and striving to the last."[14]

In the wake of this brutal attack, there were several other skirmishes between the Massachusetts tribe and the settlers, in which three Indians were killed. Weston's men, probably with urging from Standish, left for Maine and from there took a ship for England. Standish, following Bradford's orders, beheaded Wituwamat and carried his head back to Plymouth, where it was displayed on a stake on top of the Pilgrim fort.

There is no incident in the story of William Bradford and the Pilgrims of Plymouth that does more to destroy the myth of the Pilgrims as "plaster saints" than this one. There is also no incident that is more troubling when looking at William Bradford's life.

It is easy now to be disgusted by the surprise attack on the Indians and by Bradford's order to bring Wituwamat's head back. Indeed, Pastor John Robinson was dismayed when he learned of the attack and placed much of the blame on the Wessagusset men. "You will say they [the Indians] deserved it," he wrote. "I grant it, but upon what provocations and invitements by those heathenish [men at Wessagusset]?" He also questioned Standish's abilities as a leader, wondering if, perhaps, the Captain was "wanting that tenderness of the life of man . . . which is [proper]." Then, in a sentence that

Bradford surely saw as a rebuke, the Pilgrim pastor reminded the governor: "It is also a thing more glorious, in men's eyes, than pleasing in God's or convenient for Christians, to be a terrour to poor barbourous people."[15]

Indeed, Bradford may well have been swayed in making his plans by Standish, who had a notoriously short fuse when threatened. Still, the decision to kill the Indians was William Bradford's and his alone.

In Bradford's defense, if the Indians had successfully attacked Wessagusset, Plymouth would almost certainly have been their next target. Since Plymouth could only have armed about fifty men to defend the settlement against a large army of Massachusetts Indians and their allies, the Pilgrims undoubtedly would have been wiped out. At the same time, as Bradford considered how to deal with the threat from the north, he must have recalled the deaths of the four hundred English settlers in Virginia just a short time before. He knew he had to take whatever action he thought was necessary to protect Plymouth from the same fate.

Winslow, a good friend to the Indians, was troubled by the attack but viewed it as a necessary evil. "[W]e knew no means to deliver our countrymen and preserve ourselves, than by turning their [the Indians'] malicious and cruel purposes upon their own heads, and causing them to fall into the same pit they had digged for others," he wrote, adding that it "much grieved us to shed the blood of those whose good we ever intended and aimed at, as a principal [sic] in all our proceedings."[16]

The idea of taking Wituwamat's head as a trophy is repugnant to us today, but in the early seventeenth century, such displays were commonplace. Indeed, London Bridge was regularly decorated with the heads of executed men and women, and the severed body parts of executed traitors and murderers were routinely sent to towns across England where they were put on display to show English men and women what could happen to those found guilty of serious crimes.

In the final analysis we can't say with certainty whether the attack was justified or not. For all we know, if Standish and his men had not killed the Indians, Plymouth Colony might be no more than a footnote to America's history. What we do know is that the attack achieved its immediate goals. The threat to Plymouth was ended.

Bradford, though, must have been uncomfortable about the killing of the Indians. His history, painstakingly complete about most of the colony's day-to-day affairs, contains no mention of the attack on Wituwamat and the others. It is as if he found the whole episode so troubling that he simply refused to admit it ever happened.

In any event, other matters soon filled William Bradford's mind. Plymouth might be safe from Indian attack, but the colony was still being threatened, and it was his job to protect the community that was his beloved family.

THE END
OF COMMUNISM

*"All this while no supply was heard of, neither knew
they when they might expect any. So they began to
think how they might raise as much corn as they
could, and obtain a better crop than they had done,
that they might not still thus languish in misery."*[1]

Not long after the attack on the Indians at Wessagusset,
a bedraggled and haggard European entered Plymouth
and asked to speak to the governor. It was Thomas
Weston, the Merchant Adventurer who had arranged
financing for the Pilgrims and been a constant thorn in
their sides.

According to Bradford, while the Pilgrims had been
struggling to survive in America, Weston was having
his own difficulties. His shady financial dealings had
attracted the attention of the Council for New England,
the government body that was in charge of the New
England Colonies, and he had been warned to stay away
from their territory. Never one to pay too much attention to rules, Weston, in early 1623, had journeyed to

New England disguised as a blacksmith and using a phony name. After his arrival in Maine, he learned that Wessagusset had been disbanded. Wanting to see for himself how things stood, he headed for Massachusetts with two companions.

They were shipwrecked, cast ashore, and captured by Indians, who, Bradford said, "pillaged him of all he saved from the sea, and stripped him out of all his clothes to his shirt."[2] Somehow, Weston escaped his captors and managed to make his way to Piscataqua, the settlement known today as Portsmouth, New Hampshire. From Piscataqua, he walked to Plymouth.

Given the problems that Weston had caused the Pilgrims, it would have been understandable if Bradford had been pleased to see the sudden change in his fortunes. Instead, he was able to find a moral lesson in the troubles of the reckless speculator. "A strange alteration there was in him, to such as had seen and known him in his former flourishing condition; so uncertain are the ... things of this unstable world," Bradford wrote. "And yet men set their hearts upon [these uncertain things] though they daily see the vanity thereof."[3]

Meanwhile, even though he was half-naked and penniless, Weston was still a fast-talking deal maker. He asked Bradford and the other Pilgrim leaders to give him beaver pelts that he could use in trade. In payment, he promised to give them "anything . . . they stood in need of" as soon as a supply ship he expected arrived in New England.[4]

Bradford knew that Weston made empty promises and knew as well that if he and the other Pilgrim leaders lent Weston pelts there would, in Bradford's words, be "a mutiny among the people" of Plymouth. Still, the Pilgrim leaders decided, almost certainly at Bradford's urging, to lend him about one hundred skins but to keep the transaction secret from the other settlers. This "loan" was made, Bradford said, because he "pitied [Weston's] case, and remembered his former courtesies."[5]

Not surprisingly, Weston responded to the Pilgrims' generosity with ill will. He not only never repaid the loan but also gleefully spread the news that Bradford and the other Pilgrim leaders–supposed paragons of virtue–had made a secret loan to him without consulting the other settlers.

Coming so soon on the heels of the attack on the Indians at Wessagusset, Bradford's kindness to the undeserving Weston seems almost contradictory. In reality, though, these two episodes simply show that Bradford, like all men and women, had many sides. He could be harsh, even brutal, when it came to dealing with those who threatened his beloved "family" at Plymouth. He could also be compassionate and forgiving and loyal. Indeed, his compassion and loyalty would later endanger the colony he loved so dearly.

Meanwhile, by the time of Weston's visit in the spring of 1623, Plymouth was again facing the threat of famine. Not only were the settlers running short of food, but they had used some of their seed corn to feed the starving men at Wessagusset. With the planting season fast approaching, Bradford knew drastic steps would have to be taken to guarantee a good harvest, for the colony simply could not survive another winter without adequate food.

The trouble, Bradford believed, lay in the fact that the agreement between the Pilgrims and the Merchant Adventurers called for the settlers to work for "the general good" instead of for themselves. This experiment in what we would call communism was just not working. Young, unmarried men resented the fact that they had to work for other men's wives and children. Women didn't like cooking and washing for the unmarried men. Those who worked hard and produced good crops got the same rations as the lazy. This situation, Bradford said, "was found to breed much confusion and discontent and retard much employment that would have been to their benefit and comfort."[6]

After seeking the advice of "the chiefest among them"–including, no doubt, Allerton, Brewster, and Standish–Bradford announced that each family would be assigned a portion of farmland according to its size, that single boys and youths would be assigned to family units, and that from that time on every man should raise his own corn and other crops.

From mid-April until the end of May, the Pilgrims were busy planting. Men, women, and children, Bradford noted, went willingly to work in the fields that had been given to each family by the colony. The new arrangement, he said, "had very good success, for it made all hands very industrious, so as much more corn was planted than . . . by any means the governor or any other could use. . . ."[7]

It takes time for planted crops to grow. After planting their seed corn and beans, the storehouse where the Pilgrims kept supplies was empty. "All their victuals were spent," Bradford said, so that they went to bed at night "not many times knowing where to have a bit of anything [to eat] the next day."[8] Their situation was made worse by the fact that the Indians, frightened in the wake of the killings at Wessagusset, were reluctant to visit Plymouth to trade.

Desperate for food, the Pilgrims, who had never been successful as fishermen, had to depend on the sea if they were to survive. Bradford took charge. He divided the men in the colony into several companies of a half-dozen or so men each. He sent these companies to sea in the shallop according to a regular schedule, under orders not to return without fish for the colony's tables. On days—and there were many—when no fish were caught, most of the Pilgrim men, women, and older children ranged along the sandflats that lay just off what is now Plymouth Beach, digging for clams and mussels. One or two of the stronger men hunted in the woods near the settlement where, Bradford said, "they got now and then a deer," whose meat was shared by all in the colony.[9]

After the planting the Pilgrims—like farmers everywhere—prayed for gentle rains and plenty of sunshine, knowing their very survival depended on a good harvest. Day after day, they looked anxiously at the sky, hoping and praying to see dark, rain-filled clouds. But day after day, they saw nothing but a blue sky and a bright sun, for New England that year experienced a drought. By the middle of July it appeared that all their hard work in planting was in vain.

Looking at the corn struggling to survive without water must have filled Bradford and the others with terror. The crops hung limp and dry from a lack of water, Edward Winslow wrote, "changing the color in such manner, as we judged it utterly dead." The Pilgrims, he added, "were overthrown, and we discouraged, our joy being turned into mourning."[10]

To Bradford it seemed that the drought was punishment from God for something the Pilgrims had done or left undone. What he called "a solemn day of humiliation" might restore them to God's favor.[11]

At his order, a day was set aside so they could "humble [themselves] together before the Lord by fasting and prayer." All in the colony, both Saints and Strangers, assembled in the meeting room in the fort on Fort Hill. As they marched up the hill, the sky overhead was clear and, Winslow said, "the drought as likely to continue as ever it was. . . ."[12]

For eight or nine hours the Pilgrims prayed. By the time they started back down the hill, "the weather was overcast, the clouds gathered together on all sides. . . ." Miracle of miracles, at least to the Pilgrim minds, "the next morning distilled such soft, sweet, and moderate showers of rain, continuing some fourteen days, and mixed with such seasonable weather, as it was hard to say whether our withered corn, or drooping affections, were most quickened or revived."[13]

For two weeks, the soft and gentle rain continued. The planted crops grew green and began to flourish. At about the same time, Captain Standish returned from a successful trading voyage with sorely needed provisions. Suddenly, it seemed that Providence was once again smiling on Plymouth. "For which mercy," Bradford noted, "they also set apart a day of thanksgiving." It is likely that this Thanksgiving Day was celebrated on July 30, 1623. The Pilgrims, in fact, never did have a regular Thanksgiving Day, though a law passed in 1636 allowed the governor and his assistants "to command solemn days of humiliation by fasting, etc., and also for thanksgiving as occasion shall be offered."[14]

In early August, not long after that day of thanks, a ship sailed into Plymouth Harbor. Within minutes, as word of the ship's arrival spread, settlers dropped what they were doing and rushed to watch as the vessel rounded into the wind and slid to a halt.

This ship was the *Anne*, one of two vessels sent by the Merchant Adventurers with additional settlers and supplies for the colony. Quickly, the *Anne*'s crew lowered a ship's boat, and about sixty passengers made their way to shore. Excited Pilgrims searched the faces of the newcomers, hoping to catch sight of loved ones they had left behind in England or Holland. Shouts of joy rang out as families were reunited. The Brewsters' daughters Patience and Fear clambered ashore; and the wife and five daughters of Richard Warren, a Stranger.

Bradford must have been nervous and excited as he stood on shore watching as the newcomers made their way to land. Some time earlier, when either the *Mayflower* or the *Fortune* had departed Plymouth for England, he had sent a letter asking a woman named Alice Southworth to join him in America to be what we might call a "mail-order bride." Alice was a widow whose first husband was a friend of Robert Cushman, the man who had been so instrumental in arranging Plymouth's financing. She and Bradford undoubtedly had known each other before the Pilgrims sailed for America. Now, as the *Anne*'s passengers stepped ashore, he must have been hoping that she had agreed to his written proposal. Suddenly, as the passengers stepped ashore, he spied her.

Once again, we can only imagine how Bradford felt when he and Alice met on the shores of Plymouth. They must have been elated to see each other. He, after all, had cared enough for her to ask her to marry him, and she had crossed the dangerous ocean to be his wife.

Meanwhile, any joy that Bradford and the other Saints felt as the *Anne*'s passengers came ashore was tempered when they learned that John Robinson, their beloved pastor, was not one of the passengers. The newcomers to Plymouth, on the other hand, were, in Bradford's words, "much daunted and dismayed" when they saw the conditions on shore. "Some," he added, "wished themselves in England again; others fell a-weeping, fancying their own misery in what they saw now in others; others pitying the distress they saw their friends had long been in. . . . [I]n a word all were full of sadness." It was small wonder those on the *Anne* were moved, Bradford noted, for the Pilgrims "were in a very low condition; many were ragged in apparel and some little better than half naked."[15]

A few days after the *Anne*'s arrival, a second ship, a small pinnace (a two-masted ship often used as a coastal vessel) named the *Little James*, sailed into the harbor. Sent by the Adventurers for the settlers to use as a fishing vessel, she carried about thirty passengers. Once again, we can be sure, there were joyous reunions followed by tears as the newcomers realized how bad the situation was onshore.

The arrival of these new settlers almost doubled Plymouth's population. As with the passengers on the *Mayflower*, most of the ninety-three newcomers were Strangers and most were children. Included in this number were ten men who had been sent over "on their Particular."[16] That meant they had paid their own way to New England, and that while they were to live in Plymouth, they were not required to do any work for the benefit of the colony, other than to place one bushel of Indian wheat into the common store each year.

In addition to the passengers, the *Anne* and the *Little James* delivered a letter to Bradford from Cushman, who was acting as the colony's representative in England.

In that letter, Cushman apologized for not sending more supplies and for sending Strangers who were "none of the fittest" men.[17] Indeed, Bradford was not impressed by the Strangers or by those he called the "Particulars." Some of the Strangers, he said, "were so bad as they were [obliged] . . . to send them home again the next year."[18] As for the Particulars, they were filled with dreams of fancy homes and wealth that quickly "proved castles in the air."[19]

The weeks immediately following the arrival of the *Anne* and the *Little James* were busy. Homes had to be built for the newcomers, while crops were tended and cargo—including clapboard and furs—was loaded on the *Anne* for shipment back to England.

In the midst of this busy time, on August 14, Bradford and Alice Southworth were married in a civil ceremony in the great room of the Governor's House in the center of Plymouth Town. Isaac Allerton, Bradford's assistant, almost certainly performed the ceremony in which the bride and groom entered their names in a record book which, unfortunately, was lost many years ago.

We don't know for sure how William and Alice looked on that day. We can be sure, however, that the governor wore one of his most colorful outfits, perhaps his lead-colored suit topped by his violet cloak. Alice undoubtedly wore what she would have called her "best clothes" for the celebration, probably the dark dress she wore to church, with a bit of lace at her neck and wrists and a fancy underskirt that peeked through where the front of her gown was open and turned back slightly.

One of the many guests at the ceremony was Emmanuel Altham, a Merchant Adventurer and an admirer of the Pilgrims who had come to Plymouth on the *Little James*. In a letter to his brother, he described the wedding in terms that made it plain that Bradford and the other Pilgrims enjoyed a good party when they had the opportunity.

"Massasoit was sent for to the wedding, where came with him his wife, the queen, . . . four other kings (probably subchiefs) and about six score men with their bows and arrows. . . . [W]hen they came to our town, we saluted them with the shooting off of many muskets. . . ." Massasoit brought three or four bucks and a turkey to help feed the guests and entertained with dancing, "with such a noise that you would wonder. . . ." The wedding guests enjoyed venison "pasty," a kind of meat pie, and "other such good cheer" that included, Altham said, "the best grapes that ever you [saw]—and the biggest and divers sorts of plums and nuts. . . ."[20] Though he didn't mention drink, it is safe to assume that several toasts were drunk to the bride and groom.

Not long after Bradford's marriage to Alice, the *Anne* departed for England heavily laden with beaver skins, clapboard, and spices. Edward Winslow, Bradford's trusted adviser, sailed as a passenger on the *Anne* with instructions to let the Adventurers know the state of the colony. He also had instructions from Bradford to ask that Pastor Robinson be sent to Plymouth immediately, and that no more Strangers or Particulars be sent.

By the time the *Anne* departed in late August, the crops were ready to harvest. As the Pilgrims swarmed across the colony's fields gathering the fruits of their labor, it was clear that Bradford's decision to allow the settlers to work for themselves had been the right one. The harvest gathered that fall was bountiful. Heavy bushels of corn, beans, and Indian askutasquash (known today as squash) were hauled from the fields. "[I]nstead of famine now God gave them plenty, and the face of things was changed, to the rejoicing of the hearts of many, for which they blessed God." Indeed, Bradford said, "general want or famine hath not been amongst them since [then] to this day."[21]

With the bountiful harvest gathered, Bradford must have been able to relax a bit. Perhaps he took the time to become better acquainted with his new wife, Alice, or to sit and read some of the books he always treasured. Whatever he did, though, his time of ease did not last very long.

In mid-September, Captain Robert Gorges came to Plymouth. Gorges, the son of Sir Ferdinando Gorges, who was a member of the Council for New England, brought a shipload of colonists and a patent to settle what had been Weston's land in Wessagusset. In addition, he was armed with a commission from his father's Council for New England naming him the "general governor of the country."[22] That commission meant that Plymouth was now under the control of young Gorges and that Bradford would be nothing more than an assistant.

Somehow, Bradford found the good grace to make Gorges and his men welcome, seeing to it that they were "kindly entertained" by the Pilgrims.[23] Still, he must have found it difficult, especially when he discovered that Gorges had brought with him an Anglican minister who had what Bradford called the "power and authority of superintendency" over the church in Plymouth.[24] This minister, the Reverend William Morrell, embodied the very interference from England that Bradford and the other Pilgrim leaders had always feared.

Gorges also came armed with an order to arrest Thomas Weston on charges he had cheated the Council for New England by selling supplies that the council had purchased for the Wessagusset settlement. Just at that moment, Weston, who seemed to be plagued by bad luck, reappeared at Plymouth.

Though Weston had long been an irritant to Plymouth, Bradford once again showed his capacity for forgiveness and compassion in his dealings with him by helping him gain his freedom. Luckily for the colony, soon after being freed, Weston sailed for Virginia, taking with him several of the Particulars who had come to Plymouth earlier in the year.

Gorges, meanwhile, did not remain long in New England. By the spring of 1624, he was tired of Massachusetts and took ship for England with some of his settlers. "The Governor," Bradford wrote, referring to Gorges, ". . . returned for England . . . not finding the state of things here to answer his quality and condition."[25]

The Reverend Morrell, the Anglican minister, was one of those who accompanied Gorges back to England. Perhaps because he was impressed by the Pilgrims, or perhaps because he simply saw it would be foolish to try to enforce his "superintendency" over the Saints, his presence in the colony had caused no difficulties.

In March 1624, not long after Gorges's departure, it was once again time to elect a governor for the colony. For three years, Bradford had served his Pilgrim family as their leader and father figure. He was weary. He wanted someone to take his place. "If it was any honor or benefit [to serve as governor]," he said, "it was fit others should be made partakers of it; if it was a burthen . . . it was but [fair] others should help bear it. . . ."[26]

The other settlers would not let Bradford rest. Once again, he was elected governor, although the voters did provide him with five assistants to help lighten some of his burdens.

The simple fact was that, as far as the settlers were concerned, there was no other man they would trust as their leader. At the age of thirty-four, Bradford had proved his worth by governing the little settlement through its toughest times. Now, as they were beginning to reap the rewards of all their courage and faith and sweat, was not the time to change leaders.

Bradford bowed to the will of the people. He must have thought his next year of service would be easier. He would quickly discover just how mistaken he was.

✺ 13 ✺

TRIBULATIONS, TRIALS, AND A NEW BEGINNING

*"It pleased the Lord to give the Plantation peace
and health and contented minds, and so to bless their
labors as they had corn sufficient,
and some to spare. . . ."*[1]

Not long after William Bradford's reelection as governor in the spring of 1624, the trading vessel *Charity* dropped anchor in Plymouth Harbor. On board was Edward Winslow, returning from his mission to London. He brought with him much-needed supplies for the colonists, including goods that could be used for trading with the Indians. He also brought, at Bradford's request, three heifers and a bull, which Bradford called "the first beginning of any cattle in the land."[2]

The *Charity* also carried several letters, including one from Robert Cushman in England. In his letter, Cushman apologized to Bradford for not sending "such comfortable things as butter, sugar, etc." He explained there simply was not enough money to pay for such luxuries.[3] However, the Merchant Adventurers shipped fishing gear to the colony, hoping that the Pilgrims could support themselves as fishermen. In addition, they had hired and sent to Plymouth a boatbuilder who was to construct a fleet of fishing boats; and a saltmaker, supposedly expert in curing cod. Eventually, the boatbuilder proved good at his craft, although he died before he was able to complete plans to outfit the settlement with a fleet of fishing vessels. The saltmaker, on the other hand, proved to be a braggart who never did produce any salt to speak of.

Cushman's letter also advised the Pilgrims to be more discreet when they wrote to their friends and loved ones in England. Some in the colony, he noted, described Plymouth as a paradise on earth, while others "say you are starved in body and soul . . . that you eat pigs and dogs that die alone." These letters, he said, cause "passionate humors" in the Adventurers, whose willingness to support the colony was waning fast.[4]

Another letter, from Robert Sherley, one of the Adventurers who happened to be a strong backer of Plymouth, included a list of objections raised against the Pilgrims and Plymouth by Particulars who had returned to England full of complaints. Some of these complaints had to do with the way the colony was run. Others had to do with the character of the Pilgrims. The Particulars also griped that the water in Plymouth was unhealthy and that all the settlers were tortured by mosquitoes. "I pray you consider [these objections]," Sherley wrote, "and answer them by the first conveniency."[5]

Bradford's answers, sent back to England on board the *Charity*, were short and to the point. He refuted each charge in a tone that made it clear he considered the claims of the Particulars to be ridiculous. At the same time, his answer to complaints that the water was not wholesome showed that his sense of humor was still intact. "If they mean, not so wholesome as the good beer and wine in London (which they so dearly love)," he wrote, "we will not dispute with them; but . . . for water it is as good as any in the world. . . ." He went on to say that men who were bothered by mosquitoes were "too delicate and unfit to begin new plantations." Such people, he added, should "keep at home till at least they be mosquito-proof."[6]

At about this time, Bradford was approached by the settlers who wanted to be given permanent ownership of their own plots of land. The experience of the prior year had taught him that the settlers produced more corn when they worked for themselves. He quickly agreed to the settlers' request. "And to each person was given . . . one acre of land, to them and theirs, as near the town as might be. . . ," he wrote.[7]

Meanwhile, as Bradford went about his business as governor, a crisis as serious as any that had ever troubled the settlement was brewing in Plymouth Town. This crisis centered around the Reverend John Lyford, an Anglican minister who had been dispatched to Plymouth on the *Charity* by the Adventurers, many of whom were staunch Church of England men.

On its face, Lyford's presence in Plymouth was an insult to Bradford and the other Pilgrim Saints who had undergone so many trials to separate from the Anglican Church and its ministers. Bradford and the others must have been enraged that their financial backers dared to send Lyford to Plymouth while refusing to send their own pastor, John Robinson. Still, from his first day in the settlement, Lyford was made welcome. He was given a fine house and, Bradford said, "a larger allowance of food . . . than any other had" to feed himself, his wife and five children.[8]

Lyford, for his part, seemed willing to do almost anything to fit in with the Pilgrims. "When this man first came ashore," Bradford said, "he saluted them with . . . reverence and humility . . . , and indeed made them ashamed, he so bowed and cringed unto them, and would have kissed their hands if they would have suffered him."[9]

Lyford quickly ingratiated himself with Bradford and the other Pilgrims when he expressed a desire to become a member of the Plymouth church. He also confessed to what he called "disorderly walking" in his past—something the Pilgrims thought meant practicing the Anglican faith.[10] In a short time, he not only was accepted into the Plymouth church, but was also invited to join Brewster and Bradford's five assistant governors as a member of what was known as the Governor's Council.

While Lyford was solidifying his place in Plymouth, John Oldham, a Particular who had come over on the *Anne* and remained after the others returned to England, came forward to beg the forgiveness of the Saints. In his time in the colony, he confessed, "he had done them (the Pilgrims) wrong by word and deed, and (by) writing (complaints) into England."[11] Now, Oldham said, he was ready to change his ways. Bradford, who seems always to have been willing to think the best of a man when it came to matters of faith, accepted Oldham at his word, welcomed him to the fold, and also made him a member of the council.

Soon, the governor must have wondered why he ever trusted both Oldham and Lyford, for the two men almost immediately began plotting together and with others—including John Billington, that constant trouble-maker—to overthrow Bradford and turn Plymouth into an Anglican colony.

Such underhanded actions were hard to hide in a tiny place like Plymouth, and Bradford soon saw that Lyford spent hours writing what seemed to be lengthy letters. When he wasn't writing, he was often whispering with Oldham and Billington and others, sharing, in Bradford's words, "such things as made them laugh in their sleeves."[12]

Bradford may have been a loving father-figure ready to forgive erring members of the Plymouth family, but he was also an adept politician. He knew that a conspiracy was being hatched. He suspected that Lyford was writing unfavorable reports to friends in London. And he knew that if such reports made it into the hands of the Council for New England, Plymouth could be stripped of its status as a colony.

Forewarned, Bradford showed just how wily he could be. When the *Charity*, which had gone north on a fishing expedition, called again at Plymouth before re-turning to England, he watched as Lyford and Oldham gave the ship's captain a large bundle of letters for de-livery in London. On the day the ship set sail, Bradford followed in a shallop with several of his loyal friends. Overtaking the *Charity*, he and his friends boarded her and quickly found almost two dozen letters sent by the conspirators. According to Bradford, the letters were full of lies. He and his friends, working for several hours, made copies of the letters, then returned to Plymouth.

There, he and the others kept silent while they waited, as Bradford said, for "things to ripen that they might better discover [the conspirators'] intents."[13]

Bradford did not have to wait long. Thinking they had gotten away with sending false reports to England, Oldham, Lyford, and the others soon began causing trouble. Called to guard duty, Oldham refused to come, argued with Myles Standish, drew his knife, and called the hot-tempered Standish some uncomplimentary names, including "a beggarly rascal." Bradford had Oldham put in the fort lockup until he calmed down and then waited for Lyford to show his hand.

Finally, Lyford did the unthinkable—at least as far as the Saints were concerned—when he brazenly held an Anglican service in violation of the colony's rules. Bradford immediately summoned all the freemen in the colony to a court at which he charged Lyford and Oldham with "disturbing the peace, both in respect of their civil and church state. . . ."[14]

Bradford's conduct of the trial was pure theater. Without revealing he had copies of their letters, he told the men what they were charged with. When Lyford acted as if he had been wronged, Bradford produced the letters and began to read them. Lyford could only stand in silence. Oldham, on the other hand, leapt to his feet and tried to exhort his cronies to action. "My masters, where is your hearts?" he cried. "Now show your courage, you have oft complained to me. . . . Now is the time, if you will do anything, I will stand by you. . . . "[15]

For a moment, all in the meeting room must have held their breath, for they were armed just as they would be at church services. Standish and others who were firmly behind Bradford stood with their muskets and swords at the ready. Had any man moved to join

Oldham, the scene could have become bloody in an instant. Instead, Bradford reported, "not a man opened his mouth, but all were silent. . . ."[16]

Convicted of what amounted to treason, both Oldham and Lyford were banished from Plymouth. Oldham was ordered to leave at once, though his family was allowed to stay until he was able to care for them somewhere else. Lyford, who begged forgiveness, was allowed to stay for six months with the understanding that if his conduct improved his sentence would be revoked.

The trial and conviction of the two would-be traitors did not end the trouble they caused. Lyford behaved himself for a time, but once again began to write letters to England complaining of matters in Plymouth. When his six months of probation ended, he was forced to leave the colony. The Pilgrims were well rid of him, since they later discovered that his troublemaking in Plymouth was nothing compared with his activities in England and Ireland, where he had a history of molesting his wife's maids.

Oldham, on the other hand, stayed away from Plymouth until the annual election in March 1625 when, once again, Bradford was named governor of the colony. Returning to Plymouth at that time, Oldham ranted and insulted Bradford and the other settlers until he was again locked in the jail on Fort Hill. Released the next day, he was forced to pass between two ranks of musketeers. "[E]very one," Bradford said, "was ordered to give him a thump on the breech with the butt end of his musket. . . ."

With his bottom sore, Oldham was then taken to the waterfront, where a boat was waiting to carry him away. "Then," Bradford said, "they bid him go and mend his manners." Eventually Oldham did reform himself to such an extent that he was allowed to visit Plymouth as he pleased.[17]

Meanwhile, despite its political difficulties, Plymouth was flourishing. Crops were planted, tended, and harvested. The yield was good enough that the Pilgrims were able to trade again. It appeared that the little settlement truly was on a firm footing at least as far as its food supply was concerned. Bradford, at about this time, wrote a letter to Cushman in which he described the colony in glowing terms. The Pilgrims, he said, "never felt the sweetness of the country 'till this year; and not only we but all planters [colonists] in the land begin to do it."[18]

Just when Bradford and the other Pilgrims might have had a chance to breathe more easily, news of their dealings with Lyford and Oldham reached the Adventurers in London. To many of those financial backers who had lost money on their investment in Plymouth, the treatment given to the minister they had sent to the colony was the last straw. These Adventurers would have no more to do with the Pilgrims. Others, however, who believed in the Pilgrim ideal of founding a God-centered community in America, wanted to continue supporting Plymouth even if they never earned any profits from the venture. Torn by dissension, the group that had been brought together by Weston broke apart.

In an effort to salvage relations with their financial backers, Bradford quickly dispatched Myles Standish to London sometime in 1625. Though the captain was not able to accomplish much in England, which at that time was ravaged by the plague, he did begin negotiations that would ultimately enable the Pilgrims to become the owners of their own colony.

When Standish returned from England early in 1626, however, he brought terrible news. John Robinson, the Saints' dearly loved pastor and the source of much of their spiritual strength even though he had never set foot in Plymouth, was dead. The news of his death, Bradford said, "struck them with much sorrow and sadness. . . ." Another piece of bad news that Standish brought was that Robert Cushman, described by Bradford as "their ancient friend . . . who was as their right hand," had died, probably of the plague.[19]

Cushman's death was a terrible blow to his son, Thomas, who had been part of Bradford's household since 1621 when he was left in Plymouth by his father. As Bradford tried to comfort nineteen-year-old Thomas, he probably thought of his own son, John, who, for some reason, was still in Holland. He must have remembered how he himself had felt as a young boy, orphaned and alone. Perhaps he felt guilty because he had not yet sent for John, who by that time was eleven years of age. We will never know, however, for Bradford's history of Plymouth contains no reference to John at all. But we do know that not long after learning of the deaths of Cushman and Robinson, Bradford made arrangements for his son to come to the colony and that young John arrived in Plymouth sometime in 1627.

Sadly, William Bradford and his son were destined never to be close. In Plymouth the boy became part of a crowded and busy household that included Bradford; his wife, Alice; William Bradford, Jr. (born to Alice in 1624); Thomas Cushman, who was adopted by Bradford following his father's death; and several other children left orphans during the sickness of 1621. There was no way that William and his son could make up for the seven years that they had spent apart.

John Bradford himself never played any role in the story of Plymouth, although he lived in the colony until 1645. He died in 1660, without having any children of his own.

Meanwhile, Isaac Allerton went to London to try to work out some agreement with the Adventurers so that the Pilgrims and their backers knew exactly what their rights and claims were. Instead, Allerton made a deal whereby the Adventurers promised to sell the colony outright to the Pilgrims for 1,800 pounds—equal to about $300,000 in today's money—in nine payments of £200 each year. In exchange, the Pilgrims would finally be their own masters.

The bargain that Allerton made with the Adventurers marked the beginning of a new era in Plymouth. Suddenly, though they were saddled with a mortgage, the colonists owned all they had worked so hard to create. This ownership, however, raised some questions. How, for example, would the assets of the colony be divided? Would Strangers be included as owners? Including the Strangers as property owners seemed only fair to Bradford and his assistants, since they had "borne their parts in former miseries and wants with them [the Saints]."[20] In addition, the Pilgrims knew they needed men for defense and, perhaps most important, that a failure to include the Strangers in the ownership of the colony could lead to strife and even bloodshed.

To that end, it was decided that each single man or head of a family—Saint or Stranger—would be what was known as a "purchaser." Each purchaser was given 20 acres (8 hectares) of land and a house. A cow and two goats—part of a herd purchased from a failed English settlement at Monhegan Island in Maine—were also given to every six of the purchasers.

At the same time, Bradford and the other Pilgrim leaders organized a group known as the Undertakers. These eight men—including Bradford, Brewster, Allerton, Winslow, Standish, John Alden, Thomas Prence, and John Howland—were to "undertake" the payment of the £1,800 mortgage held by the Adventurers and an additional £600 or so owed to other lenders. The Undertakers also would import necessities from England—shoes, leather, shot and powder, nails, medicines, spices, and so on—which they would trade to the settlers for corn at a guaranteed rate. In exchange for these services, they were granted a six-year monopoly in trade with the Indians. They could do what they liked with the furs, corn, beads, knives, and other trade goods in the common storehouse. They alone had the use of Plymouth's trading posts and boats. Profits after they paid the colony's debts would be theirs.

This arrangement seems to have favored the Undertakers, but the financial burden that Bradford and the others agreed to carry was substantial. Indeed, Bradford said, "they knew not well how to raise the payment and discharge their other engagements and supply the yearly wants of the Plantation."[21] Still, it must have seemed to Bradford that he and the other members of his Pilgrim family at Plymouth were finally going to be able to enjoy the fruits of their labors. Sadly, this was not the case.

❦ 14 ❦

INTO THE BRIARS

"Mr. Allerton doth . . . wholly now desert them;
having brought them into the briars, he leaves
them to get out as they can."[1]

It is easy to imagine Bradford in those days climbing to
the top of Fort Hill to stand looking down on Plymouth
Town, the tiny community that was his surrogate family. No doubt he gave thanks to God. At the same time,
he must have felt a least a twinge of pride as he gazed
over the thirty-two houses that made up the town, the
enclosed gardens, and the neat fields that provided corn
and other food to the settlers.

By that time, it had become clear to Bradford that
Plymouth would never thrive as a fishing community.
The Pilgrims were able to catch fish for their own use,
but every time they tried to establish fishing as a money-
making business, they failed. Indeed, the colony's attempts to profit from fishing were so dismal that
Bradford described the trade as "a thing fatal to this
plantation."[2]

Saddled with the huge debt they owed to the Merchant Adventurers, Bradford and the other Undertakers had to find a way to earn profits. At that time, and for many years after, beaver and otter, both in plentiful supply in New England, were in great demand in England, where pelts were used to make coats and hats worn by upper-class men and women.

The Indians, as Bradford had learned during a trading voyage with Squanto in 1621, were happy to barter cured pelts to the Pilgrims for "truck," including blankets, tools, bowls, and other merchandise purchased in England and shipped to Plymouth. While the cost of buying and transporting trade goods was considerable, the value of pelts was high enough to make the business profitable. At a time when a working man in England earned about a shilling a day—one-twentieth of an English pound—each beaver pelt sold for about twelve shillings and an otter pelt for roughly ten shillings.

Once Bradford decided that the colony should focus on the fur trade to earn money, he moved quickly. On his orders, a fur trading post was established at a spot the Indians called Aptucxet, on Buzzards Bay, where the "arm" of Cape Cod joins the mainland of Massachusetts. Not long after that, a second post was established at Kennebec, in Maine.

Meanwhile, Dutch settlers had been gaining a foothold on the Hudson River to the south. There, in 1626, they established the colony of New Amsterdam (New York). Peter Minuit, the governor of the Dutch settlement, knew of the Pilgrim colony to the north and wanted to establish trade with his English neighbors. In 1627 he sent a letter addressed to the "Noble, worshipful, wise, and prudent Lords, the Governor and

*A trading party. This image reminds us of the
caution with which Native Americans and the colonials
must have approached each other.*

Councillors residing in New Plymouth, our very dear friends."[3] In that letter, Minuit invited the Pilgrims to begin trade with New Amsterdam. Bradford, who had liked the Dutch since his time in Holland, replied with a friendly letter of his own, one that must have impressed the Dutchmen, since he wrote to them in their own language. However, he told the Dutch the Pilgrims had "all necessaries, both for clothing and other things" they needed, at least for the next year.[4]

The Dutch were not put off by Bradford's answer. In October 1627, just a few months after the exchange of letters between the two governors, Minuit sent Isaak de Rasieres, the chief trader, or *Opper Koopman*, of New Amsterdam, to Plymouth. De Rasieres brought with him sugar, as well as linen and other cloth made in Holland. What was of the greatest interest to Bradford and the other Pilgrims, however, was something the Dutchman said the Indians called *wampumpeag*. This word, de Rasieres explained, meant "white strings of money" and was usually shortened to *wampum*.[5]

This strange form of money came in two types, black and white. The white, made from the polished stems of periwinkles (seashells), was about twice as valuable as the black, which was fashioned from the inside of clam shells. Polished and drilled to form little cylinders, wampum was strung on parallel strings to form belts that were then used just like currency.

Bradford and the Pilgrim leaders were skeptical about the usefulness of wampum. Finally, though, they were persuaded to buy £50 worth of what they must have thought was nothing more than funny money. At first, it seemed that the Pilgrims had been cheated by the Dutch. The Indians around Plymouth were not much interested in trading beaver or otter pelts for wampum. "[I]t was two years before they could [trade] this small quantity," Bradford wrote, "till the inland people knew of it; and afterwards they could scarce get enough for them. . . ."[6]

As the Indian demand for wampum increased, the Pilgrim trade with the Wampanoags, the Massachusetts, and the tribes in Maine and on Cape Cod flourished. Indeed, since the Pilgrims had access to the only supply of wampum in the region, they enjoyed a virtual monopoly of the fur trade for several years.

It is from de Rasieres, meanwhile, that we have the best description of Plymouth as it was in the late 1620s. "New Plymouth," he wrote in a letter to a friend in 1628, "lies on the slope of a hill stretching east towards the sea-coast, with a broad street about a cannon shot of 800 feet [244 meters] long, leading down the hill; with a [street] crossing in the middle, [and running southwards] to the rivulet and [northwards] to the land. The houses are constructed of clapboards, with gardens also enclosed behind and at the sides with clapboards, so that their houses and courtyards are arranged in good order, with a stockade against sudden attack."[7]

De Rasieres was particularly impressed by Plymouth's government and the fact that the Pilgrims, under Bradford's leadership, had passed laws against fornication and adultery, "which laws they maintain and enforce very strictly indeed, even among the tribes which live amongst them."[8]

In the wake of de Rasieres's visit, trade between the Pilgrims and the Dutch flourished. At the same time, furs flowed into the colony from trading posts established in outlying areas. Bradford must have believed, perhaps for the first time, that the Undertakers would be able to pay their debt to the Adventurers as scheduled. Indeed, in mid-1628, he sent his longtime assistant, Isaac Allerton, to England with a cargo of furs large enough to reduce the Undertakers' total indebtedness by about £300.

Bradford should have been able to relax a bit in those days as the colony began to flourish. However, it seemed that Plymouth and its governor would never know a time without a crisis, for even as the colony's financial outlook improved, trouble arose on a different front. This had its origins in 1625 when a Captain Wollaston, about whom nothing is known with certainty, his business partner Thomas Morton, and about thirty-five indentured servants established a tiny settlement near what had been Weston's plantation at Wessagusset.

By early 1627, Wollaston had tired of life in New England. He left the little settlement he had called Mount Wollaston and departed for Virginia with some of his servants. In Virginia, he discovered he could sell his servants' indentures (contracts) to tobacco planters for a healthy profit. He quickly sent a message to Morton asking him to send the rest of the indentured servants to him without delay.

Morton, a lawyer and, it is thought, a graduate of Oxford, was also a rogue. Rather than send the servants to Virginia as instructed, he invited them to a feast, plied them with what the Pilgrims described as "strong drink," and then made them an offer they couldn't refuse. Forget about Wollaston, he said, and "I will receive you as my partners and consociates; so you may be free from service, and we will converse, plant, trade, and live together as equals and support and protect one another. . . ."[9]

The servants, of course, jumped at Morton's offer to enjoy a life of leisure and frolic instead of a life of labor in Virginia. In this way what was probably the strangest settlement in America's history was born. One of Morton's first acts was to rename the little plantation "*Mare Mount*," a mix of Latin and English meaning "Mountain by the Sea."

There, Morton and his "consociates" soon raised a maypole around which they sang and danced and frolicked with sailors from any ships that happened by, with Indian braves and—much to the chagrin of the Pilgrims—with Indian maidens. They had themselves such a grand time that the Pilgrims began calling the settlement "Merrymount."

Morton said that what went on at Merrymount was no more than "harmless mirthe by young men,"[10] but Bradford and the other Pilgrims viewed the dancing and frolicking as sinful. Morton, Bradford wrote, was the "Lord of Misrule"; his settlement nothing better than "a school of Atheism."[11]

For a time, it appeared that the Pilgrims would simply have to tolerate their rowdy neighbors. Then, however, Morton began trading liquor, muskets, and powder and shot to the Indians. This not only decreased the value of the Pilgrims' comparatively tame trade goods, but also put weapons in the hands of Indians who might decide to drive the English from their lands at any time.

The seriousness of this situation was soon realized not just by the Plymouth settlers but also by a handful of other English settlers who had founded a half-dozen or so small, scattered plantations in Massachusetts in the years since the arrival of the Pilgrims in 1620. In the spring of 1628, Bradford reported, these settlers asked him to use Plymouth's resources to stop Morton's foolishness. Eventually, seven small plantations, in addition to Plymouth, contributed to a "war chest" to finance some action against Morton.

Before taking action, Bradford and the leaders of these outlying settlements sent several warning messages to Morton, who responded insolently. By mid-1628, Bradford and the others had had enough of Morton and his cohorts. It was time to act. Captain Myles Standish was dispatched with a force of nine men to deal with them.

What is now known as the Battle of Merrymount was more of a minor skirmish than a battle. According to Standish, Morton and his men locked themselves in a house with plenty of weapons. When asked to surrender, they responded with jeers and laughter. They might have put up a real fight, had they not been so drunk that they could not aim their heavy muskets. Morton, armed with a smaller firearm, rushed at Standish, who easily knocked his weapon aside and took him captive. After being exiled to an island near the coast for several months, he was shipped back to England in late 1628.

Some scholars have pointed to the clash between Morton and the Pilgrims to prove that the Pilgrims were "blue noses"—moralists who couldn't stand to see anybody have a good time. The facts, however, show that while Bradford and the other Saints found Morton's behavior scandalous, they attacked him because he was putting guns in the hands of Indian warriors. Bradford saw that what was going on at Merrymount was a danger to the Pilgrim family under his care. Just as he had done at Wessagusset when the colony was threatened, he took action.

Meanwhile, even as Bradford took steps to remove Morton, another threat to Plymouth's future was unfolding. This time, though, the threat did not come from Strangers, outsiders, or Indians. It came instead from Isaac Allerton, one of the Saints and one of Bradford's trusted assistants.

By the late 1620s, Allerton had been handling the colony's business affairs in England for several years. During those years, he carried thousands of pounds' worth of furs to England to pay the Undertakers' debts. He purchased supplies for the colony's trading posts. He represented the settlement in negotiations with English officials, first to obtain a larger grant for land along the Kennebec River in Maine where the Pilgrims had a trading post and later to obtain a royal charter for the colony of New Plymouth. He was in a position to do great good for the colony, or great harm.

The first hints of trouble came in 1628. At that time, it became apparent to Bradford and the other Undertakers that Allerton had a bad habit of mixing his own business affairs with those of the colony. He shipped merchandise for his own use as a trader mixed in with the truck that the Undertakers needed to trade with the Dutch and Indians. Only he knew which was which. And, Bradford noted, ". . . what was most vendible [salable] and would yield present pay" was his, while the remainder belonged to the Undertakers.[12] Still, Bradford and the other Undertakers—unwilling to believe that one of the Saints could be a crook—did not look too closely.

That changed in 1630, after Allerton returned from one of his frequent trips to England bearing the royal charter he had been instructed to obtain. This charter, known as the Warwick Patent because it was signed by the Earl of Warwick along with Sir Ferdinando Gorges, made William Bradford the trustee for the colony, placing all its lands at his disposal. It also granted to Plymouth all the land in New England southeast of a line drawn roughly from the lower shore of Boston Bay to the head of Narragansett Bay. In addition, it granted the Pilgrims a strip of land about 15 miles (24 kilometers) wide along both sides of the Kennebec.

All this was wonderful, except for one problem. While the patent was signed by Gorges and the Earl of Warwick, it did not bear the Great Seal of the English king, Charles I. Without that seal the patent was not legal. Bradford soon discovered that the king had refused to sign because Allerton, acting on his own, had inserted a clause in the patent exempting Plymouth from the payment of customs duties (taxes) on imported goods for seven years and on exported goods for twenty-one years. Since the Undertakers had spent £500—a small fortune—to obtain the patent, Bradford was understandably furious.

Even that misstep by Allerton, however, might have been overlooked. But he made a much more serious mistake when he brought Thomas Morton, the "Lord of Misrule," back with him from England to serve as his assistant. While Morton was soon persuaded to leave Plymouth, Allerton's behavior caused Bradford and the other Undertakers to take a long, hard look at how he had been conducting their business.

Simply stated, they discovered that Allerton was a cheat and a thief. His thievery was hidden behind a tangle of complicated business dealings that was, as Bradford said, ". . . not ended till many years after, nor well understood of a long time, but folded up in obscurity and kept in the clouds, to the great loss and vexation of the Plantation. . . ."[13]

To account for every crooked thing Allerton did in his career as the colony's business agent would fill a book. Indeed, Bradford devotes many pages in his history discussing what he referred to as Allerton's "affairs." Essentially, instead of paying the debts that Bradford and the other Undertakers owed to the Adventurers, Allerton stole hundreds of pounds. He charged the Pilgrims twice for some merchandise he purchased, and took exorbitant fees from the Undertakers for his expenses in England.

How was it possible for Bradford to place so much trust in a man like Allerton? In fact, how could he continue trusting him with the colony's business affairs even as he investigated Allerton's dealings and began to find evidence of his thievery?

The answer to those questions lies in Bradford's personality and character and beliefs. While he was ready to deal harshly with Plymouth's enemies, he was unflaggingly loyal to those who served him and the colony he loved. He proved that in the colony's early days when Massasoit wanted to execute Squanto. At the same time, Bradford was kind even to those who turned against him, as he showed in his behavior to Thomas Weston when he appeared in Plymouth Town half-naked and destitute.

In looking at the way Bradford reacted to Allerton's treachery, it should be noted that he was almost unable to believe that one of the Saints would dare break his covenant with the Pilgrim community and the Pilgrim church. To Bradford this covenant was a holy bond, an agreement among the Saints as a group and between the Saints and their God. It was the foundation on which the Saints had constructed their unbreakable church and their godly "civil body politic." Breaking this holy promise was not just an offense against the Plymouth family, but a slap in the face of God.

There was another reason, as well, which Bradford described as a "more secret cause." Allerton, he noted, "had married the daughter [Fear] of their Reverend Elder, Mr. Brewster, a man beloved and honored among them . . . whom they were loath to grieve or in any way offend. . . ."[14] This second motivation must have been particularly strong in Bradford's case. Brewster, after all, was the man who had taken him under his wing, the man who had been like a father to him.

Finally, though, Bradford and the other Undertakers had no choice but to admit to themselves that Allerton had, indeed, broken his covenant. In fact, when an accounting was finally made and Allerton was discharged from his post as the colony's business manager, it was discovered that the Undertakers–who thought their debt to the Adventurers had been greatly reduced–still owed £1,000 on their mortgage. What was worse, they discovered that the scattered debt that amounted to about £600 in 1627 had swelled to an amazing £4,770 in 1632!

Included in that debt was about 500 pounds Allerton spent in 1627 to pay for the transport of two shiploads of settlers from Leyden to New England. The first of these ships arrived late that year, bearing about thirty-five men, women, and children. It is likely that it was this vessel that carried young John Bradford to Plymouth. The second ship carried about sixty settlers, who seem to have been haphazardly gathered by Allerton. These settlers included many non-Saints, who apparently were not well-suited for life in Plymouth. Indeed, they made so little impact on the colony that no record was made of their names or of what became of them in the New World.

Remarkably, even after Allerton's abuse of the Pilgrims, Bradford was able to find charity and forgiveness for his friend and helper in his heart. As Bradford himself said, Allerton had provided many years of "good and faithful service" to the colony.[15] It is not likely he set out to cheat the Undertakers or the Pilgrims. Instead, he was a good man tempted by a chance to make some easy money. At least for a time, he probably believed he could get away with his actions without hurting anyone in the colony. "With pity and compassion touching Mr. Allerton," Bradford wrote, "I may say with the Apostle to Timothy . . . , 'They that will be rich fall into many temptations and snares, . . . and pierce themselves through with many sorrows, . . . for the love of money is the root of all evil.'"[16]

Sadly, though, while Bradford was able to find forgiveness in his heart for Allerton—the trusted Saint and the signer of the Mayflower Compact who became a traitor—it took the Undertakers about two decades to completely pay off all the bills he had run up in their names. And Bradford and the others were only able to clear their indebtedness after they sold some of their property in Plymouth to raise money.

Allerton, meanwhile, was allowed to remain in the colony, though he no longer served in any official capacity. His wife, Fear, died in 1633, at which time he moved, eventually making his way to New Amsterdam. By 1645 he was established as a merchant in the young and rapidly growing town of New Haven in Connecticut. There Allerton appeared to prosper, building a large house. He died in 1659. It would have come as no surprise to Bradford that Allerton's seeming wealth was false and that he had, in fact, died insolvent, owing many who had, like Bradford and the Undertakers, trusted him.

Meanwhile, even before Allerton's treachery began, events transpiring in England would change Plymouth Colony forever. By 1629, when Bradford and the other Undertakers began to suspect Allerton's double-dealing, what might be called the best of times and the worst of times in Plymouth Colony were about to begin.

❦ 15 ❦

THE COST OF PROSPERITY

*"Those that had lived so long together in
Christian and comfortable fellowship must
now part and suffer many divisions."[1]*

During the early 1630s as William Bradford and the
other Undertakers worked to rid themselves of the
crushing debt incurred by Isaac Allerton, Plymouth
Colony began to thrive in ways none of the Pilgrims
could have foreseen.

The colony's sudden prosperity came about because
of political changes that swept across England while
Plymouth's settlers were struggling to create their God-
centered community in Massachusetts. During the
1620s, as King James I died and was replaced by his
son, Charles I, the political power and influence of the
Puritans was on the increase.

Frightened by the power wielded by the Puritans,
who questioned the authority of the crown not just in
religious matters but in civil matters as well, the king
fought back. In fact, Charles I seemed bent on making
good on his father's promise to "harry" the noncon-

formists out of England. Puritans were jailed, stripped of their property, fined, and, in some cases, executed because their democratic views supposedly threatened the English crown.

As early as 1628, some of these Puritans decided—as the Scrooby Pilgrims had done twenty years earlier—that the only way they could escape the wrath of the English authorities was to emigrate. At first, just a few left England to move to lands near Plymouth Colony. Under the leadership of John Endecott, a small settlement was established at Salem, and an even smaller one near what is now Boston.

As the political situation in England worsened, more and more Puritans determined to flee to the New World. One of those who did was a highborn, well-educated lawyer named John Winthrop. In 1629, Winthrop joined a group of wealthy Puritan men who had formed a company—the Massachusetts Bay Company—to establish a new colony north of Plymouth. Soon, he was chosen to lead the efforts to found the colony.

Under Winthrop's leadership, a flotilla of four ships left England in the spring of 1630. This was the vanguard of what we know today as the great Puritan Migration. Unlike the Pilgrims' move to the New World in 1620, the Puritan Migration was no haphazard undertaking of just a hundred or so undersupplied men, women, and children heading for the wilderness. The ships under Winthrop's command carried four hundred settlers, both Puritan and non-Puritan. This first wave of immigrants was followed almost immediately by a second fleet carrying an additional six hundred men, women, and children. These settlers quickly established themselves on the banks of the Charles River, naming their city Boston.

During the next dozen years, a steady flow of Puritan ships loaded with supplies, building materials, and settlers, including craftsmen and craftswomen of every sort, crossed the Atlantic to Massachusetts Bay. Between 1630 and 1642, when the migration ended, more than 14,000 settlers moved to what was known as the Massachusetts Bay Colony. By comparison, during the first decade of Plymouth's history, its population grew from about one hundred to about three hundred.

William Bradford saw this great Puritan Migration as a victory for the Pilgrims. The Pilgrims, after all, had paved the way for the Puritans. They had proved, where others had failed, that an English settlement could survive in New England. That victory became sweeter, when, not long after their arrival, the Puritans adopted the Pilgrim style of democratic church for their own churches in the New World.

When informed that the Puritan churches were being modeled on that of Plymouth, Bradford was filled with joy, though he was careful to give proper credit to God. "Thus out of small beginnings," he wrote, "greater things have been produced by His hand that made all things of nothing. . . . [A]s one small candle may light a thousand, so the light here kindled hath shone unto many, yea in some sort to our whole nation. . . ."[2]

From documents that have survived, it is clear that William Bradford of Plymouth and John Winthrop of Massachusetts respected each other. In his journal, Winthrop described Bradford as "a very discreet and grave man,"[3] while Bradford said that Winthrop was among the "ablest gentlemen in the Bay of the Massachusetts."[4] Though Bradford respected Winthrop, however, he also realized almost immediately that the stronger, better-situated, and better-financed Puritan colony

John Winthrop, governor of Massachusetts Bay Colony

posed a threat to Plymouth's future and, as time passed, the two men were often at loggerheads as each tried to protect his territory.

The first contact between the two governors was by letter when, in late 1630, Bradford was faced with a legal problem he apparently did not feel qualified to handle on his own. At that time, John Billington, the settler who had been a troublemaker since Plymouth's early days, the same man who had cursed and quarreled with Captain Standish, was found guilty of murdering a fellow settler and sentenced to death.

Faced with the responsibility of ordering Billington's execution, Bradford wrote to Winthrop. Perhaps Bradford was squeamish at the thought of killing a man who had made the voyage on the *Mayflower* and who had affixed his name to the Mayflower Compact. Perhaps he wasn't sure of his own judgment when it came to executing a settler he undoubtedly did not care for. In any event, Winthrop quickly "concurred with them that he ought to die."[5] Accordingly, in September of 1630, Billington was executed. Though we don't know for sure, it is likely that he was hanged and that the execution was carried out by Standish.

The first face-to-face meeting between the governor of Plymouth and the governor of Boston took place not long after Billington's execution when Bradford traveled north to Boston to greet Winthrop's wife, who had just arrived in the Bay Colony.

After this first meeting, the two governors frequently corresponded, usually about charges that Plymouth was encroaching on the lands or interfering with the business of the Bay Colony, or vice versa. In early 1632, for example, Winthrop wrote to Bradford complaining that one of the Bay Colony settlers, a man named John Pickworth, had moved from Boston to Plymouth. Boston's leaders, it was believed, were worried that their settlers might be lured to Plymouth, where the rules were less rigid. Bradford, once again showing the wit that often marked his writing, answered that Pickworth had come to Plymouth to work for a few weeks, had found a young woman to marry, and decided to stay there. Pickworth, Bradford went on, was happy in Plymouth, having "no cause to complaine, excepte he hath [got] a bad wife."[6]

Meanwhile, the rapid and steady settlement of the Bay Colony, as the Puritan settlement was properly called, gave Plymouth's economy a boost. Many of the Puritan settlers were comparatively wealthy. They provided a ready market for corn and for the cattle that the Pilgrims had been raising since Winslow brought the first bull and three heifers to the colony in 1624. Prices for both corn and animals soared, for demand was great and supply limited. By 1638 a milk cow was selling for as much as £25, the equivalent of about $4,000 in today's money. A milk goat fetched £3 or £4, and a bushel of corn sold for 6 shillings. The Pilgrims, used to barely surviving, now had money.

There was, though, a downside to the rapid growth of the Bay Colony. For more than a decade, Plymouth Town—as tiny as it was—had been the largest settlement in New England. After 1630, in what must have seemed like the blink of an eye, it was eclipsed by Boston. Trading vessels that once called at Plymouth now bypassed the town and sailed on to Boston. Settlers that might have moved to Plymouth Town instead were drawn to Boston with its greater opportunities and comforts.

At the same time, the sudden demand for corn and cattle meant that the Plymouth settlers needed more land than they had been granted when the Undertakers divided the colony's holdings among the freemen and their families. Suddenly, Plymouth's settlers began moving away from the town that had been so laboriously built by Bradford and the other Old Comers, as he called those who came to Plymouth on the *Mayflower*. What Bradford had always feared—the scattering of the Pilgrim family and church, the tearing apart of the tight-knit town that embodied the dream of the Saints—had started.

Within a year of the arrival of the Puritans, several of Plymouth Town's most famous residents—including Myles Standish, the colony's military leader and a stalwart friend to Bradford; Jonathan Brewster, the elder Brewster's son; and John Alden, the Stranger who gained fame as the man who fell in love with and married Priscilla Mullins—moved northeast, to the opposite shore of Plymouth Harbor. There they established the settlement of Duxbury, probably originally called "Ducks-burrow" in honor of the thousands of seabirds that lived in the shallow water near its shores. In 1632 this group received permission from the Plymouth Church to establish the First Church of Duxbury.

During the next several years, six additional towns, including Scituate and Marshfield, were settled on Plymouth Colony lands but away from Plymouth Town. These new towns attracted settlers not just from England and from the Bay Colony but also from Plymouth Town. The town that once had been the only successful English settlement in New England was soon little more than a distant suburb of Boston. In fact, while Boston's population was soaring in the decade of the 1630s, that of Plymouth Town actually declined.

Bradford was dismayed by what he saw happening to the colony he loved. "And no man now thought he could live except he had cattle and a great deal of ground to keep them . . . ," he wrote. "By which means they were scattered all over the Bay quickly and the town in which they had lived compactly until now was left very thin and in a short time almost desolate."[7]

The scattering of new settlements in Plymouth Colony, meanwhile, led to changes in the way Plymouth was governed. For years, government had been a kind of informal affair. Laws were written only when they were needed. By 1636 it was obvious that this system was no longer workable. Accordingly, in that year, Bradford, his assistants, and representatives from Duxbury and Scituate wrote a formal body of laws known as the "General Fundamentals" or "Declaration of Rights." Approved by the Freemen at the General Court, as the main governmental body was known, the General Fundamentals were similar to the Bill of Rights that were drawn up almost 150 years later when the United States of America was born.

The Fundamentals stated that no laws could be made or taxes levied without "the consent of the body of freemen or associates, or their representatives legally assembled. . . ."[8] According to the Fundamentals, there was to be an annual election of the colony's governor and assistants, with all the Freemen eligible to vote. All criminal offenders were guaranteed a trial by a jury of twelve men, and any defendant in a trial could challenge any of his jurors. Civil rights were protected by a regulation that no person could be condemned or sentenced without the testimony of two individuals or without sufficient circumstantial evidence.

During these years, while the Wampanoags remained allied with the Plymouth Colony, and the Massachusetts Indians who lived near Boston were allies of the Bay Colony, the Pequots, a warlike tribe that inhabited Connecticut, resisted when white men began moving onto their lands.

Serious trouble began when an English trader named John Stone was killed, along with eight of his companions, as they were making their way up the Connecticut River. When asked to surrender the men responsible for the killings, Sassacus, the Pequot sachem, refused, claiming that Stone and his men had been killed only because they had kidnapped an Indian brave. What Sassacus claimed was probably true, since Stone had a reputation for being brutal in his treatment of Indians. In any event, Winthrop of Boston believed that the Indians responsible for Stone's death should be brought to trial.

At about the same time, John Oldham, the trouble-maker who had allied himself with John Lyford in an attempt to take over Plymouth, was killed at Block Island, off the south shore of Rhode Island, supposedly by Indians who then took refuge with the Pequots. Again, when Winthrop asked Sassacus to surrender those responsible for the attack, the Indian chief refused. Winthrop decided to act. He quickly sent Captain John Endecott—the Bay Colony's military leader—with about forty armed men to the Connecticut River to teach the Indians a lesson.

Endecott proved to be a heavy-handed teacher. Landing on the shores of the Connecticut, he killed a number of Pequot—including women and children—and set fire to their lodges. He then returned to Boston, leaving the settlers on the Connecticut frontier to face the understandable rage of the Pequots.

In early 1637 the Pequots began to exact their revenge. They attacked settlers as they hunted or worked in their fields and fell on traders as they made their way up the Connecticut. Soon, Winthrop was begging Bradford to help wage war on the Pequots. Reluctantly, Bradford and the other leaders of Plymouth agreed they would send about fifty armed men to join in an expedition against the Indians.

As it turned out, the Plymouth men were delayed by contrary winds when they tried to sail around Cape Cod to join the force assembled to do battle with the

Pequots. Instead, a combined "army" of men from Connecticut and Massachusetts along with some Narragansett braves surrounded the Pequots' main village near the mouth of the Mystic River and attacked without warning. The Indians, armed only with bows and arrows, had no chance against the heavily armed white men. In a matter of moments, the Indian village was ablaze. About four hundred Pequot men, women, and children died in this bloody attack.

"It was a fearful sight," Bradford wrote, apparently based on an eyewitness report, since he was not there, "to see them thus frying in the fire, and the streams of blood quenching the same, and horrible was the stink and scent thereof."[9]

About two hundred Pequot women and eighty Indian men who survived the first attack fled from their village and took refuge in a nearby swamp. All but a handful were killed, and those who survived were sold into slavery. The proud Pequot people never fully recovered from the brutal attack. Sassacus himself somehow escaped and made his way to a Mohawk Indian village, where he was promptly murdered. His head was shipped to Boston, where it was no doubt displayed as a trophy of war and a warning to other Indians who might have ideas about resisting the settlers.

Bradford felt that the settlers in the Bay Colony bore some responsibility for this short-lived and tragic "war." Still, he said, "the victory seemed a sweet sacrifice, and they gave the praise therefore to God."[10]

In looking at Bradford's response to the annihilation of the Pequots, we are forced again to acknowledge that he was not a perfect man—at least not by our standards. Capable of friendship with Squanto and able to build a trusting relationship with Massasoit, he could also give praise to God for the eradication of the Pequots.

They were, in his mind, a threat not just to Connecticut but to all of God's chosen people who had come to settle in New England. Therefore, to Bradford's way of thinking, the eradication of the Pequot people was predetermined. It was the will of God and, therefore, right and proper.

Meanwhile, as Connecticut and the Bay Colony dealt with the Indians to the west, Bradford had his own problems to deal with much closer to home. Freemen, those who had moved from Plymouth Town to distant townships and newcomers who had been granted land, began complaining that it was inconvenient to travel to town for the three meetings of the General Court held each year. Though Bradford must have seen this as nothing more than additional evidence that Plymouth Town was being torn apart, he knew he had no choice but to act in response to those complaints. At about the same time as the Pequot War, a representative form of government was established in Plymouth Colony. Freemen in the towns of Barnstable, Duxbury, Sandwich, Scituate, Taunton, and Yarmouth each elected two representatives, while Plymouth Town elected four, to serve as "deputies" at meetings of the General Court.

The scattering of the town's population posed yet another problem for Bradford. Thanks to the patent that Allerton had brought to America in 1630, Bradford was, in a technical sense, the "owner" of Plymouth Plantation's lands. That meant he had the legal right to decide who would receive grants of land, and where. Bradford wanted to keep Plymouth a tightly knit, God-centered community. That meant he preferred to keep power in the hands of the Old Comers, and to do that, he guarded the colony's land to keep it out of the hands of people or groups who did not fit in with the ideals of the Saints. Early in 1639, though, many of the Freemen of the now-scattered colony were complaining that Bradford had too much control. At the General Court in March of that year he was challenged to explain why no large tracts of land had been granted to any of the newcomers.

Bradford could have gotten angry, and he would have been justified. For two decades, he had served the colony unstintingly and without pay. Instead of reacting angrily, however, Bradford made the colony's Freemen an offer. In exchange for two or three large plots of land to be given to himself and the other Old Comers, and up to £300 to be paid to him and his fellow Undertakers if they needed the money to pay their debts, he would surrender to the Freemen all the rights, privileges, and benefits of the patent. The Freemen quickly accepted Bradford's offer.

In surrendering his patent, William Bradford turned his back on a chance to become a wealthy, powerful man, the ruler of his own minikingdom in America. Though he never explained why he so willingly gave up the patent, he probably saw this as a diplomatic move that would stop conflict between the Old Comers, who held much of the land, and the newcomers, who were jealous. And to his way of thinking, the survival of Plymouth was much more important than money or power.

Sadly, the survival of Plymouth as a unified, Christian community seemed less likely as the decade of the 1630s ended and the 1640s began. The Pilgrim diaspora—the scattering of settlers from Plymouth Town—continued. At that time, Bradford and William Brewster must often have sadly reminisced about the "old days" in Scrooby and in Holland and about the dream that had brought all the Saints to the New World in hopes of creating a commonwealth of like-minded men and women.

Then, on April 18, 1643, in the midst of his struggle to hold Plymouth together, Bradford suffered what he described as a "matter of great sadness and mourning" when his "dear and loving friend" William Brewster died at the age of eighty. "For his personal abilities, he was qualified above many," Bradford wrote not long after his friend's death. "He was wise and discreet and well-spoken . . . , of a very cheerful spirit, very sociable and pleasant . . . , of a humble and modest mind, of a peaceable disposition. . . . He was tenderhearted and compassionate of such as were in misery. . . ."[11]

In 1644, just one year after Brewster's death, affairs in Plymouth reached a low point when a group of the town's settlers proposed leaving Plymouth to move to Nauset on Cape Cod. Bradford was opposed to the idea, knowing that meant giving up once and for all the dream that had carried the Saints to the shores of Massachusetts. While the plan to move the town was later abandoned, several of Plymouth's leading families moved to the cape, where they established the town of Eastham. Suddenly, Plymouth's population was reduced to about one hundred and fifty persons, fewer than in 1623.

"And thus," Bradford wrote, "was this poor church left, like an ancient mother grown old and forsaken of her children . . . ; her ancient members being most of them worn away by death, and these of later time being like children translated into other families, and she like a widow left only to trust in God."

"Thus," he added, in what must be viewed as one of the most melancholy statements in his history of the colony, "she that had made many rich became herself poor."[12]

⬥ 16 ⬥

THE END OF THE PILGRIMAGE

"Now blessed holy Bradford . . .
Is gone to place of rest. . . ."[1]

The death of William Brewster and the dispersal of most of the settlers from Plymouth Town in the early 1640s marked, for William Bradford, the beginning of the end of his dream—the Separatist dream—of creating a family-like, Christian community in the New World. While he would continue serving Plymouth Colony for fourteen more years, twelve of those years as governor, his service now was prompted more by a sense of duty than by hope or any joyous vision of the future.

The depth of Bradford's despair at this time of his life is easy to see in the pages of his famous history, *Of Plymouth Plantation*—not in what he wrote but, rather, in what he did not write. For years, Bradford had faithfully recorded the story of the Pilgrims and Plymouth. After Brewster's death and the dispersal of the colony, his writing became perfunctory, as if it pained him to put his quill to paper. Instead of lengthy entries about each year's events, he wrote just a few words.

Still, Bradford was a busy man in those years. He served as judge, military adviser, and ambassador. He married young couples and—when not engaged in colony business—tended to his goats and cattle, cared for his extensive lands, and probably went fishing. In the evenings, when the toil of the day was done, he must have enjoyed visiting with the other Old Comers who remained in Plymouth Town, swapping stories and memories.

The Governor's House in the center of Plymouth Town must have been a bustling place in those days. Although the children from Alice Bradford's first marriage had moved out by 1637, and Thomas Cushman, who had been part of the family since his father's death in 1624, was gone a few years later, the house was still crowded. It was home not only to Bradford and his wife but also to their three children—William, Jr., Mercy, and Joseph—along with an orphaned boy the couple had taken in. Colonists and other leaders of the town must have been frequent callers, dropping in just to chat with the most respected of all the Pilgrims or to seek his advice. And though Bradford doesn't mention any visits from the Indians who lived near the town, it is likely that Massasoit, who lived until 1661, came from time to time to pay his respects.

During these years, as Bradford grew older, it would have seemed somehow proper if he had at least been able to enjoy a measure of peace and quiet. As it had been throughout its history, however, Plymouth was battered by one crisis after another. In the early 1640s, when England was on the brink of a civil war that would ultimately see King Charles I beheaded and the nation governed by the Puritans, the flood of settlers to the Bay Colony slowed and then stopped. Demand for the cattle and corn that had made Plymouth rich dried up and prices dropped. "A cow that but a month before was worth £20 . . . , fell now to £5 and would yield no more," Bradford wrote, adding that the prices slid "from the highest pitch at once to the lowest." Plymouth, awash in money for a time, was once again poor.[2]

At about the same time, Plymouth Colony's morals began to suffer, at least in Bradford's eyes. It seemed impossible, he wrote, to "suppress the breaking out of sundry notorious sins . . . , especially drunkenness and uncleanness. Not only incontinency between persons unmarried, for which both men and women have been punished . . . , but some married persons also. But that which is worse . . . [things fearful to name] have broke forth in this land oftener than once."[3]

In the midst of these troubles, the English colonists in America felt threatened by the possibility that with England torn by civil war, some unfriendly power–the Dutch or French, for example–might try to drive them from the land.

In 1643, not long after Brewster's death, the leaders of the New England colonies met at Boston, where they formed what is known as the New England Confederation. According to the articles of confederation agreed to at that time, a governing board of two commissioners each from Plymouth, Massachusetts, and New Haven, Connecticut–then a separate settlement–were to meet regularly. These commissioners (Bradford served as one of Plymouth's representatives) had the authority to declare war and call armies for both defensive and offensive purposes, with the costs of war to be shared proportionately by each colony. In addition, commissioners had authority over Indian affairs, fugitives, and disagreements between colonies.

John Quincy Adams, the Massachusetts-born president of the United States and a famous historian, wrote two centuries after Bradford's time that the idea for the New England Confederation originated in Plymouth. It may have been that the idea of forming a union of the New England colonies came from William Bradford, who had seen such a confederation at work in the United Netherlands. In any event, when Bradford and the leaders of the other English colonies formed their union, they established a tradition of cooperation between the colonies that would come to fruition more than a century later in the formation of the thirteen English colonies as the United States of America.

Meanwhile, Bradford suffered another personal loss in 1646 when Edward Winslow, his good friend, his coauthor in the writing of "Mourt's Relation," and his ambassador to the Indians and other settlements, returned to England. Winslow was so happy to be in a nation in the control of the God-fearing Puritans that he never returned to Plymouth.

While Winslow's decision not to return to Massachusetts must have struck Bradford as a loss not just for himself but for Plymouth, it is lucky, in a way, he decided to remain in England. There, Winslow became a fairly wealthy man, enough to have his formal portrait painted in 1651. As far as we know, this is the only authentic portrait ever made of a Pilgrim. In it, Winslow is dressed in a dark doublet with gold buttons, ruffled sleeves, and a high, white collar held in place by a tasseled gold chain. What appears to be a gold signet ring is on the little finger of his right hand. His hair hangs to his collar, and he sports a neatly trimmed mustache and small, pointed beard. If nothing else, this portrait puts to rest the idea that Pilgrims wore only drab clothes and no jewelry. Winslow's portrait also gives us the only hint we have about how William Bradford might have looked, since it is likely he dressed and wore his hair and beard much as Winslow did. As far as we know, Bradford himself never sat for a portrait. If he was ever given the opportunity he almost certainly would have refused.

Having written just a few lines about the events of 1646 and a few lines about Winslow's departure, William Bradford saw no reason to continue keeping a record of an experiment that, in his mind at least, had failed. "*Anno* 1647," he wrote at the top of a blank page, indicating the beginning of a new year (*anno* in Latin). "And *Anno* 1648," he wrote beneath that first entry, presumably a year later.[4] But under those dates he wrote no more about the Pilgrims of Plymouth.

It is easy to imagine Bradford bent over his writing table in the great room of the Governor's House in the heart of Plymouth, staring down at the pages of that journal with his quill in hand, his eyes filled with the sad tears of a suddenly old man who believed that he had wasted his life chasing a dream that proved to be nothing but that—a dream without substance.

By 1648, Bradford was complaining of bad health, using "bodily infirmities" as an excuse not to attend a meeting where he and Winslow were to have arbitrated a dispute between the Dutch in New Amsterdam and English settlers in New Haven.[5] This was the first time since his sickness during the Pilgrims' earliest days in Plymouth that Bradford was ill, as far as we know. The boy Cotton Mather described as a sickly child had led a remarkably healthy life. At the age of fifty-eight, however, he was beginning to tire, to feel the ravages of time.

Still, Bradford continued serving as governor, although there is virtually no record of what he did during the next several years. At the age of sixty, he took up the study of Hebrew, wanting, he said, to study "that most ancient language, and holy tongue, in which the Law and oracles of God were writ; and in which God, and angels, spake. . . ."[6]

And though he did not add to his history of the colony, except for a list of the *Mayflower*'s passengers added sometime after 1648, he did write poetry and essays about spiritual matters.

During these years, Bradford and Alice probably settled into a comfortable routine. Their house–the governor's "mansion"–had undoubtedly been enlarged over time, probably with the addition of a second story and additional rooms. The hand-hewn furniture of the colony's earliest days was replaced with "store bought" items shipped from England to America, including a beautiful carved chair currently on display at Plymouth Plantation. From what little is known, he and his wife seem to have loved each other deeply. In her will, Alice requested that when she died she be buried as close to William as might be convenient, surely not the request of an unloving or unloved wife.

We do know of one event in Bradford's later years that says a great deal about his character. In 1650 an unexpected visitor came to Plymouth. This visitor was Father Gabriel Druillettes, a member of the Roman Catholic order known as the Society of Jesus, or Jesuits. Priests of this order had a long history of fighting against the Reformation of the Catholic Church in England and throughout Europe. Because of that history, they were considered little better than devils by most Protestants, including, no doubt, Bradford himself.

Still, when Bradford learned that Father Druillettes had arrived in Plymouth Town, he immediately invited the priest to dine with him and Alice. It was only after he made his invitation that Bradford realized that it was a Friday, a day when Catholics were required not to eat meat. With Alice's help, and maybe even a quick fishing trip, he managed to procure a cod or some other fish for the priest's meal. In that simple act of hospitality and graciousness we see William Bradford at his very best, a man tolerant enough not only to entertain someone he must have considered his spiritual enemy but also willing to go out of his way to see that his guest was made comfortable.

Meanwhile, as time passed, Bradford certainly knew he was nearing the end of his own long pilgrimage. In May 1653 he was again sick, unable to don his ceremonial robe and take his usual seat at the General Court, even though the meetings were held in the governor's home. During the next few years, he grew weaker and was frequently ill. In late March 1657 he was again forced to miss the meeting of the General Court. On May 7 of that year, he took to his bed. The next day, he made his will.

An inventory of Bradford's estate showed that he had not allowed his desire to walk with God to stand in the way of amassing some earthly goods. Indeed, he was the richest man and largest property owner in Plymouth in 1657, with an estate valued at about £900, or the equivalent of about $135,000 in today's money. Included in his estate were many items we think of as commonplace and not very valuable: such articles as blankets, a green rug, and tablecloths. The inventory also included several muskets as well as a great beer bowl valued at £3. Also listed in the inventory was a wine cup, mute testimony that Bradford enjoyed a drink, in moderation. The list of his clothing—then so valuable that it was usually bequeathed to a relative or loved one—showed that he liked to wear colorful outfits. It included a suit with black breeches and a red waistcoat, the lead-colored suit with silver buttons he may well have worn when he and Alice were married, a black coat, a green gown, a violet cloak, one black and one colored hat, a light-colored cloak, six pairs of shoes, and two pairs of stockings. In addition he owned several books, including religious texts by Martin Luther and John Calvin, a geography book, and two Bibles.

Neither his inventory nor his will made any mention of what Bradford referred to as his "scribbled writings"—the book we know today as *Of Plymouth Plantation.* Yet this book was to prove to be his greatest and most enduring legacy, a volume considered one of the greatest books of colonial history ever written.

As William Bradford lay in bed in the inner room of the Governor's House in Plymouth on May 7, he surely knew it was his deathbed. His mind must have been filled with memories. Perhaps he remembered a snatch of song he heard when he was a boy in Austerfield. Perhaps he recalled the words of the first Puritan sermon he heard so long ago in Babworth. Perhaps he remembered the sounds and smells of the squalid hold of the *Mayflower* as she struggled across the storm-tossed Atlantic. In the dim light of his life's sunset, perhaps he closed his tired eyes and saw those who waited for him in eternity: Dorothy, his child-bride . . . and Squanto . . . and Standish, who had died not long before. As his own life came to a close, he must have been visited by Pastor Robinson . . . and William Brewster, his friend and teacher.

At about nine o'clock in the evening of May 8, 1657, William Bradford died.

He was buried on Fort Hill (now known as Burial Hill), lowered into a grave as a volley of musket shot was fired into the Plymouth sky. He was widely mourned, for, as Cotton Mather later wrote, Bradford was "lamented by all the colonies of New England as a common blessing and a father to them all."[7]

Though William Bradford died believing himself a failure, events were to prove how wrong he was. To be sure, Plymouth never became the ideal spiritual community that he and John Robinson and William Brewster and the other Saints had dreamed of. In fact, Plymouth was eventually gobbled up by the much stronger and richer Bay Colony. In the long run, however, the ideas and ideals of Plymouth—embodied in its democratic, separate church and the democratic government that grew from that church—would ultimately have more of an impact on the formation of America as we know it today than the basically aristocratic and theocratic ideals of the Puritan Massachusetts Bay Colony.

George Willison, a historian and the author of *Saints and Strangers*, a history of Plymouth Plantation, described Bradford as "talented and indefatigable, passionately devoted to the welfare of New Plimoth, . . . unquestionably the greatest of the Pilgrims, one of the greatest figures of seventeenth century New England—indeed, of our whole colonial period."[8]

William Bradford, the Rock of Plymouth, however, is all too often overlooked when the tale of the settling of America is told. Yet this "genuine Christian and consummate politician," as Samuel Eliot Morison described him, has much to say to us today, not just in the words of his history, but in the way he lived his life.[9]

❧ CHRONOLOGY ❧

1590 William Bradford is born, probably in March, in Austerfield, Yorkshire, England.

1594 William's mother, Alice, remarries. William is sent to live with his grandfather.

1596 Grandfather dies. William lives with his mother and stepfather.

1597 William's mother dies, and he is placed under the care of his uncles, Robert and Thomas Bradford.

1602 William attends his first Puritan church service.

1606 The Scrooby group is organized as a Separatist congregation with Richard Clyfton as pastor and John Robinson as teacher.

1608 About 100 members of the Scrooby group, including William Bradford, flee England for Holland.

1609 Separatists move from Amsterdam to Leyden.

1613 Bradford marries Dorothy May, daughter of an English Separatist living in Amsterdam.

1615 (?) Son John is born.

1620 Separatists, called Pilgrims for the first time, depart Holland for England (July), sail from England on board the *Mayflower* (September), and arrive at Cape Cod (November).

Dorothy, William Bradford's wife, dies.

1621 William Bradford is elected governor of Plymouth Colony.

1622 *Mourt's Relation,* based on diaries of William Bradford and Edward Winslow, is published in London.

1623 Bradford marries Alice Southworth.

1625 Pastor John Robinson dies in Leyden.

1630 Warwick Patent is issued by the Council for New England.

1637 Pequot War.

1639 Bradford surrenders ownership of Plymouth to the Freemen of Plymouth Colony.

1643 New England Confederation.

1657 William Bradford dies.

✒ Source Notes ✒

Chapter One
1. Quoted in Bradford Smith, *Bradford of Plymouth* (New York: Lippincott, 1951), 299–300.
2. Quoted in Stanley Williams, ed., *Selections from Cotton Mather* (New York: Harcourt Brace, 1926), 43.
3. Quoted in John Morrill, ed., *Oxford History of Tudor & Stuart Britain* (New York: Oxford, 1996), 126.
4. Quoted in Stanley Williams, ed., *op. cit.*, 43.
5. Revised Standard Version, Paul, 2 Corinthians 6, *Holy Bible* (Dallas, TX: Melton, 1952), 913.
6. Quoted in Stanley Williams, ed., *op. cit.*, 50.
7. Quoted in Antonia Fraser, *King James VI of Scotland–I of England* (New York: Knopf, 1975), 105.
8. William Bradford, *Of Plymouth Plantation* (New York: Knopf, 1997), 234–237.

Chapter Two
1. William Bradford, *Of Plymouth Plantation* (New York: Knopf, 1997), 10.
2. Quoted in Bradford Smith, *Bradford of Plymouth* (New York: Lippincott, 1951), 62.
3. Quoted in Stanley Williams, ed., *Selections from Cotton Mather* (New York: Harcourt Brace, 1926), 43.

4. *Ibid.*, 43.
5. Quoted in George Willison, *Saints and Strangers* (New York: Reynal & Hitchcock, 1945), 52–53.
6. William Bradford, *op. cit.*, 10.
7. *Ibid.*, 10.
8. *Ibid.*, 11.
9. *Ibid.*, 12.
10. *Ibid.*, 13.
11. *Ibid.*, 14.
12. *Ibid.*, 13.
13. *Ibid.*, 15.

CHAPTER THREE
1. William Bradford, *Of Plymouth Plantation* (New York: Knopf, 1997), 47.
2. Quoted in Mary Crawford, *In the Days of the Pilgrim Fathers* (New York: Grosset & Dunlap, 1920), 37.
3. William Bradford, *op. cit.*, 16.
4. *Ibid.*, 16.
5. *Ibid.*, 16, 17.
6. *Ibid.*, 17.
7. *Ibid.*, 17.
8. *Ibid.*, 17.
9. *Ibid.*, 24, 25.
10. *Ibid.*, 25.
11. *Ibid.*, 27.
12. *Ibid.*, 30.
13. *Ibid.*, 30.
14. *Ibid.*, 356, 357.
15. *Ibid.*, 37.
16. *Ibid.*, 47.

CHAPTER FOUR
1. William Bradford, *Of Plymouth Plantation* (New York: Knopf, 1997), 60, 61.
2. *Ibid.*, 48.
3. *Ibid.*, 48.
4. *Ibid.*, 50.

5. *Ibid.*, 55, 56.
6. *Ibid.*, 58.
7. *Ibid.*, 58.
8. *Ibid.*, 59.
9. *Ibid.*, 59.
10. *Ibid.*, 59, 60.

CHAPTER FIVE
1. William Bradford and Edward Winslow, *Mourt's Relation* (Boston: Applewood Books, 1986), 17.
2. Quoted in John Bakeless, *America as Seen by Its First Explorers* (New York: Dover, 1989), 209.
3. William Bradford, *Of Plymouth Plantation* (New York: Knopf, 1997), 60.
4. *Ibid.*, 60.
5. *Ibid.*, 60.
6. *Ibid.*, 60.
7. *Ibid.*, 61.
8. *Ibid.*, 75.
9. *Ibid.*, 370.
10. *Ibid.*, 75.
11. *Ibid.*, 75, 76.
12. Quoted in Francis Dillon, *The Pilgrims* (New York: Doubleday, 1975), 137.

CHAPTER SIX
1. William Bradford and Edward Winslow, *Mourt's Relation* (Boston: Applewood Books, 1986), 18.
2. *Ibid.*, 19.
3. *Ibid.*, 16.
4. William Bradford, *Of Plymouth Plantation* (New York: Knopf, 1997), 61, 62.
5. *Ibid.*, 64.
6. William Bradford and Edward Winslow, *op. cit.*, 20.
7. William Bradford, *op. cit.*, 64.
8. *Ibid.*, 65.
9. *Ibid.*, 65.
10. William Bradford and Edward Winslow, *op. cit.*, 21.

11. *Ibid.*, 22.
12. *Ibid.*, 22.
13. *Ibid.*, 23.
14. William Bradford, *op. cit.*, 66.
15. William Bradford and Edward Winslow, *op. cit.*, 17.

CHAPTER SEVEN
1. William Bradford and Edward Winslow, *Mourt's Relation* (Boston: Applewood Books, 1986), 38.
2. *Ibid.*, 25.
3. *Ibid.*, 25.
4. *Ibid.*, 27.
5. *Ibid.*, 27.
6. *Ibid.*, 27.
7. *Ibid.*, 31.
8. *Ibid.*, 32.
9. *Ibid.*, 34.
10. *Ibid.*, 35, 36.
11. *Ibid.*, 35, 36.
12. *Ibid.*, 37.
13. William Bradford, *Of Plymouth Plantation* (New York: Knopf, 1997), 71.
14. William Bradford and Edward Winslow, *op. cit.*, 38.
15. *Ibid.*, 38.
16. Quoted in Francis Dillon, *The Pilgrims* (Garden City, NY: Doubleday, 1975), 147.

CHAPTER EIGHT
1. William Bradford, *Of Plymouth Plantation* (New York: Knopf, 1997), 77.
2. William Bradford and Edward Winslow, *Mourt's Relation* (Boston: Applewood Books, 1986), 42.
3. William Bradford, *op. cit.*, 77.
4. *Ibid.*, 77.
5. William Bradford and Edward Winslow, *op. cit.*, 45.
6. *Ibid.*, 47.
7. *Ibid.*, 50.
8. *Ibid.*, 51.

9. *Ibid.*, 51.

10. Quoted in Alexander Young, *Chronicles of the Pilgrim Fathers* (New York: De Capo, 1971), n. 184.

11. William Bradford, *op. cit.*, 81.

12. William Bradford and Edward Winslow, *op. cit.*, 57.

13. William Bradford, *op. cit.*, 80.

14. William Bradford and Edward Winslow, *op. cit.*, 56.

15. Quoted in Alexander Young, *op. cit.*, n. 199.

16. William Bradford, *op. cit.*, 86.

17. *Ibid.*, 86.

CHAPTER NINE

1. William Bradford and Edward Winslow, *Mourt's Relation* (Boston: Applewood Books, 1986), 82.

2. William Bradford, *Of Plymouth Plantation* (New York: Knopf, 1997), 84.

3. William Bradford and Edward Winslow, *op. cit.*, 59.

4. Quoted in Alexander Young, *Chronicles of the Pilgrim Fathers* (New York: De Capo, 1971), n. 230.

5. William Bradford, *op. cit.*, 87.

6. William Bradford and Edward Winslow, *op. cit.*, 60.

7. *Ibid.*, 60.

8. *Ibid.*, 65, 66.

9. *Ibid.*, 66.

10. *Ibid.*, 67.

11. William Bradford, *op. cit.*, 99.

12. *Ibid.*, 234.

13. *Ibid.*, 90.

14. William Bradford and Edward Winslow, *op. cit.*, 82.

CHAPTER TEN

1. William Bradford, *Of Plymouth Plantation* (New York: Knopf, 1997), 101.

2. *Ibid.*, 92.

3. *Ibid.*, 92.

4. *Ibid.*, 95.

5. *Ibid.*, 96.

6. Edward Winslow, *Good Newes from New England* (Bedford, MA: Applewood Books, 1996), 15.

7. *Ibid.*, 16.

8. William Bradford, *op. cit.*, 109.

9. *Ibid.*, 110.

10. Quoted in Sydney V. James, Jr., ed., *Three Visitors to Early Plymouth* (Plymouth, MA: Plimouth Plantation, 1963), 76, 77.

11. William Bradford, *op. cit.*, 111.

12. *Ibid.*, 112.

13. *Ibid.*, 112.

14. Quoted in Sydney V. James, Jr., ed., *op. cit.*, 11.

CHAPTER ELEVEN

1. William Bradford, *Of Plymouth Plantation* (New York: Knopf, 1997), 375.

2. Edward Winslow, *Good Newes from New England* (Bedford, MA: Applewood Books, 1996), 20.

3. William Bradford, *op. cit.*, 114.

4. *Ibid.*, 116.

5. Quoted in Alexander Young, *Chronicles of the Pilgrim Fathers* (New York: De Capo, 1971), 329.

6. Edward Winslow, *op. cit.*, 35.

7. *Ibid.*, 36, 37.

8. *Ibid.*, 37.

9. William Bradford, *op. cit.*, 118.

10. Edward Winslow, *op. cit.*, 43.

11. *Ibid.*, 43.

12. *Ibid.*, 47.

13. *Ibid.*, 48.

14. *Ibid.*, 48.

15. William Bradford, *op. cit.*, 375.

16. Edward Winslow, *op. cit.*, 43.

CHAPTER TWELVE

1. William Bradford, *Of Plymouth Plantation* (New York: Knopf, 1997), 120.

2. *Ibid.*, 119.

3. *Ibid.*, 119.

4. *Ibid.*, 119.

5. *Ibid.*, 119.

6. *Ibid.*, 121.

7. *Ibid.*, 120.

8. *Ibid.*, 121, 122.

9. *Ibid.*, 123.

10. Edward Winslow, *Good Newes from New England* (Bedford, MA: Applewood Books, 1996), 54.

11. William Bradford, *op. cit.*, 131.

12. Edward Winslow, *op. cit.*, 55.

13. *Ibid.*, 55.

14. William Bradford, *op. cit.*, 132 and n. 132.

15. *Ibid.*, 130.

16. *Ibid.*, 133.

17. *Ibid.*, 128.

18. *Ibid.*, 127.

19. *Ibid.*, 133.

20. Quoted in Sydney V. James, Jr., ed., *Three Visitors to Early Plymouth* (Plymouth Plantation, MA: Plimoth Plantation, 1963), 29, 30.

21. William Bradford, *op. cit.*, 127.

22. *Ibid.*, 134.

23. *Ibid.*, 134.

24. *Ibid.*, 138.

25. *Ibid.*, 138.

26. *Ibid.*, 140.

CHAPTER THIRTEEN

1. William Bradford, *Of Plymouth Plantation* (New York: Knopf, 1997), 178.

2. *Ibid.*, 141.

3. *Ibid.*, 374.

4. *Ibid.*, 374.

5. *Ibid.*, 142.

6. *Ibid.*, 143, 144.

7. *Ibid.*, 144, 145.
8. *Ibid.*, 148.
9. *Ibid.*, 147, 148.
10. *Ibid.*, 148.
11. *Ibid.*, 149.
12. *Ibid.*, 150.
13. *Ibid.*, 151.
14. *Ibid.*, 151.
15. *Ibid.*, 152.
16. *Ibid.*, 152.
17. *Ibid.*, 165.
18. *Ibid.*, 178.
19. *Ibid.*, 179, 180.
20. *Ibid.*, 187.
21. *Ibid.*, 186.

CHAPTER FOURTEEN

1. William Bradford, *Of Plymouth Plantation* (New York: Knopf, 1997), 244.
2. *Ibid.*, 141.
3. *Ibid.*, 378.
4. *Ibid.*, 380.
5. Quoted in George Willison, *Saints and Strangers* (New York: Reynal & Hitchcock, 1945), 266.
6. William Bradford, *op. cit.*, 203.
7. Quoted in Sydney V. James, Jr., ed., *Three Visitors to Early Plymouth* (Plymouth Plantation, MA: Plimoth Plantation, 1963), 76.
8. *Ibid.*, 76.
9. William Bradford, *op. cit.*, 205.
10. Quoted in George Willison, *op. cit.*, 277.
11. William Bradford, *op. cit.*, 205.
12. *Ibid.*, 211.
13. *Ibid.*, 233.
14. *Ibid.*, 218.
15. *Ibid.*, 202.
16. *Ibid.*, 202.

CHAPTER FIFTEEN
1. William Bradford, *Of Plymouth Plantation* (New York: Knopf, 1997), 255.
2. *Ibid.*, 236.
3. Quoted in James Moseley, *John Winthrop's World* (Madison: University of Wisconsin, 1992), 57.
4. William Bradford, *op. cit.*, 234.
5. *Ibid.*, 234.
6. Quoted in Bradford Smith, *Bradford of Plymouth* (New York: Lippincott, 1951), 252.
7. William Bradford, *op. cit.*, 253.
8. Quoted in George Willison, *Saints and Strangers* (New York: Reynal & Hitchcock, 1945), 317.
9. William Bradford, *op. cit.*, 296.
10. *Ibid.*, 296.
11. *Ibid.*, 296.
12. *Ibid.*, 334.

CHAPTER SIXTEEN
1. Quoted in George Willison, *Saints and Strangers* (New York: Reynal & Hitchcock, 1945), 337.
2. William Bradford, *Of Plymouth Plantation* (New York: Knopf, 1997), 310.
3. *Ibid.*, 310.
4. *Ibid.*, 347.
5. Quoted in Bradford Smith, *Bradford of Plymouth* (New York: Lippincott, 1951), 288.
6. *Ibid.*, 306.
7. *Ibid.*, 314.
8. *Ibid.*, 320.
9. *Ibid.*, 320.

✥ BIBLIOGRAPHY ✥

WILLIAM BRADFORD'S WRITINGS

William Bradford, *Of Plymouth Plantation.* New York: Knopf, 1997.

William Bradford and Edward Winslow, *Mourt's Relation.* Boston: Applewood Books, 1986.

OTHER CONTEMPORARY WRITINGS

Richard Dunn & Laetitia Yeandle, eds., *The Journal of John Winthrop, 1630–1649.* Cambridge, MA: Harvard University Press, 1996.

Sydney James Jr., ed., *Three Visitors to Plymouth.* Plymouth Plantation, MA: Plimoth Plantation, 1963.

Edward Winslow, *Good Newes from New England.* Bedford, MA: Applewood Books, 1996.

SELECTED SECONDARY SOURCES

John Bakeless, *America as Seen by Its First Explorers.* New York: Dover, 1989.

Ezra Hoyt Byington, *The Puritan in England and New England.* Cambridge, MA: John Wilson and Son, 1896.

Thomas Fleming, *One Small Candle*. New York: W.W. Norton, 1964.

David Freeman Hawke, *Everyday Life in Early America*. New York: Harper & Row, 1989.

Ivor Hume, *Martin's Hundred*. New York: Knopf, 1982.

James W. Loewen, *Lies My Teacher Told Me*. New York: Simon & Schuster, 1995.

James Moseley, *John Winthrop's World*. Madison: University of Wisconsin, 1992.

Nathaniel B. Shurtleff, M.D., ed. *Records of the Colony of New Plymouth in New England*. Baltimore, MD: Genealogical Publishing Co., Inc., 1979.

Roland G. Usher, *The Pilgrims and Their History*. Williamstown, MA: Corner House Publishers, 1984.

Stanley Williams, ed., *Selections from Cotton Mather*. New York: Harcourt Brace, 1926.

Alexander Young, *Chronicles of the Pilgrim Fathers*. New York: De Capo, 1971.

⊛ INDEX ⊛